A TOMB WITH A VIEW

A Comedy-Thriller

NORMAN ROBBINS

SAMUEL FRENCH

LONDON
NEW YORK TORONTO SYDNEY HOLLYWOOD

ISBN 0 573 11458 7

CHARACTERS

Hamilton Penworthy
Lucien Tomb
Dora Tomb
Emily Tomb
Marcus Tomb
Anne Franklin
Agatha Hammond
Freda Mountjoy
Peregrine (Perry) Potter
Monica Tomb

The action takes place in the Library of Monument House

ACT I	Evening
ACT II Scene 1	Fifteen minutes later
Scene 2	The following morning
ACT III	That evening

Time—the present

For

FRANK and LAURA BRANDT

of

Ames, Iowa, U.S.A.

ACT I

The Library of Monument, home of the Tomb family, about fifty miles from London. Evening

The room is dominated by an immense black walnut fireplace in the centre of the rear wall. Outsize vases rest on the outer edges of the thick mantel, and in the centre stands a very heavy and ornate marble clock. Above the mantel a thick gold frame holds a terrifying portrait of the late Septimus Tomb, gaunt, wrinkled, almost bald, with the bloodshot pop-eyes of a raving lunatic. The eyes appear to follow whoever is in the room. A heavily carved wooden fender protects against sparks from the log fire, and huge fire-dogs of brass with attendant implements are in position. A thick hearthrug is in front of the fender. Massive empty bookcases, their dusty shelves protected by fine mesh doors, are built into the walls on either side of the fireplace. One of them, however, is a secret door that opens on a pivot into the room. One side wall is dominated by great french windows. Thick velvet drapes hang from a matching pelmet, and coffee-coloured net curtains obscure the view of overgrown shrubs outside. Meshed, empty bookcases fill the wall-space either side of the windows. Below the windows, slightly into the room, a small octagonal table is set. On it stand several cut-glass decanters containing various brightly coloured liquids, and a collection of glasses and goblets. Beside the table is a comfortable leather wing-chair: it is on a swivel, or easy-glide castors. In the opposite wall are massive Gothic doors of black walnut: each door has a large brass knob. These double doors form the only obvious entrance into the room. When they are open, a glimpse of the wide hall may be seen. Above the doorway is an old-fashioned roll-top writing-desk. The top is open, and a blotter, selection of quill pens, inks, papers, etc., may be seen. Papers are also crammed into the pigeon-holes and shelves. Loose envelopes lie on the floor as though spilt by accident. Above the desk is another empty, meshed bookcase, and below a small wastepaper bin. Above this an internal telephone is fixed. Below the doors, meshed, empty bookcases fill the remaining wall. Opposite the drinks table is a matching one, with a family Bible—a massive, leather-tooled tome in faded brown and gold. Just above the doorway, angled towards the drinks table, is a leather-topped library table with a library chair behind it. Ranged opposite this are eight matching dining-chairs in two rows of four, obviously brought in the for the sole purpose of the Will reading. The room is thickly carpeted. Wall lights provide an alternative to the central chandelier: both switches are by the door

When the CURTAIN *rises, the window drapes are drawn, the fire lit, and the central chandelier switched on. The room is empty, and the internal telephone is ringing furiously. After a moment it stops. A wolf howls: long and drawn out, the cry hangs in the air, then fades to silence*

The Library doors open, and Hamilton Penworthy enters. He is aged about seventy, and looks every inch the family solicitor that he is. Black tailcoat and waistcoat, gold turnip-watch with fob and chain, wing-collared shirt, pin-striped trousers and black shoes with spats. He carries a battered old deeds box which contains the Will and several other papers

Penworthy (*coughing*) Damned fog.

Still spluttering, he closes the doors, deposits the deeds box on the library table, and proceeds to the fireplace to warm his hands. As he does so, the wolf cry is repeated. Without appearing to notice, Penworthy turns from the fire and moves down to the drinks table. Surveying the decanters with a slight frown, he chooses one of the less brightly coloured liquids, cautiously sniffs at it, then pours himself a drink. The wolf howls again. Replacing the decanter Penworthy turns, picking up his glass, and gazes at the portrait of Septimus

He raises his glass

To you, Septimus. Wherever you may be. (*He chuckles*)

The wolf cry comes again. For the first time Penworthy reacts. He glances at the closed doors and shakes his head. Taking a sip at his liquid, he seats himself in the wing-chair

(*Thoughtfully*) *He* knows there's something in the wind, doesn't he? Senses it—even down there in the cellars. He's no fool, young Master Oliver. Been restless for days so they tell me—and still another week to full moon. (*He sips*)

The cry comes again, to be followed at once by the sound of an angry voice in the hall

Lucien (*off*) Quiet down there, damn you! Quiet!

Penworthy quickly knocks back the rest of his drink, puts the glass down and begins to rise

Lucien Tomb flings open the doors and struts into the room. He is an over-weight, pompous and petulant man of about fifty. Balding, myopic, dressed in ill-fitting tweeds, he is quivering with indignation

So there you are, Penworthy. Helping yourself to *my* drinks again.

Penworthy (*protesting*) My dear Mr Lucien . . .

Lucien I knew it. The moment you *refused* to answer my telephone call. What is the use of internal telephones if no-one will answer them?

Penworthy (*glancing at the telephone*) I assure you . . .

Lucien And what do you mean by telling Mrs Hammond to lay an extra place at the dinner table, eh? May I remind you that *I* am head of this household now that *that*—(*indicating the painting*)—crazy old fool is dead, and as such, *I* give the orders. If you wish to dine with us, then you ask *my* permission, family solicitor or not.

Penworthy If you'll allow me to explain . . .

Lucien (*spluttering*) There's no *need* to explain. I consider it a gross impertinence on your part, Penworthy. *Gross* impertinence.

Penworthy Nevertheless, I wish to point out that far from inviting myself to join you at the table, I was merely following the instructions of your—(*pause*) late father, that on the day of his Will reading, an additional place be set for one of the beneficiaries.

Lucien (*his eyes popping*) This is *monstrous*. I absolutely *refuse* to sit at the same table as Oliver. He was never allowed out of his cell whilst father was alive, and I don't see why we should have to tolerate him now. He should have been committed *years* ago. The day he bit off the gardener's ear.

Penworthy (*nodding*) A most distressing occurrence. (*With a quick smile*) But fortunately the poor chap was stone deaf and had no further use for it. Still—it *was* a tricky moment. (*He clears his throat*) However, that's all beside the point. The—er—the other beneficiary isn't your brother Oliver. It's a *stranger*. Someone quite unknown to the members of this family and something of an unknown quantity in herself. I'm assured though, that in the outside world, so to speak, she is something of a celebrity.

Lucien (*outraged*) You mean it's a *female*?

Penworthy (*nodding*) Miss Ermyntrude Ash, by name. A writer of romantic novels for women.

Lucien (*firmly*) Never *heard* of her.

Penworthy Nor I. But apparently your late father was very fond of her literary style, so wished to include her in his bequests as a small token of his appreciation.

Lucien She won't *accept* it, of course?

Penworthy That's entirely up to her, Mr Lucien. Naturally I wrote to her publishers, and was duly informed that she would arrive here tonight by the seven-fifteen train. I—er—I took the liberty of arranging a taxi to bring her from the station.

Lucien You're being uncommonly *free* with my money, Penworthy, if you don't mind my saying so. And how long do we have to put up with this *person*? You know how Dora feels about strangers.

Penworthy I'm afraid the duration of Miss Ash's stay at Monument House will depend on if she is willing to accept the terms of the legacy or not. She *could* be gone by tomorrow, but on the other hand . . . (*He spreads his hands*)

Lucien And what *are* the terms?

Penworthy Unfortunately I'm unable to tell you until the actual reading of the document. The terms must be explained in the full hearing of *all* parties.

Lucien (*his voice rising*) But I want to know *now*, Penworthy. I will not have perfect strangers wandering about my home, poking their noses into things that don't concern them. I won't *have* it.

Dora Tomb enters the room in a flurry of black chiffon. She is an emaciated woman of forty-nine, but could easily pass for sixty. Her hair is a grey nest, her skin like parchment, and her cheeks are over-rouged. A black chiffon scarf trails for yards behind her

Dora Won't have what, Lucien?

Lucien (*Turning to her in annoyance*) Strangers in the house. Absolute *strangers.*

Dora (*with a loud shriek of fear*) The police. (*She staggers*)

Lucien (*exasperatedly*) Don't be so *stupid.* Dora.

Dora (*clutching at him fiercely*) They were all accidents, Lucien. *Accidents.* Even the Tax Inspector. Don't let them take me.

Penworthy Miss Dora—please. *Please.* The lady concerned is quite unconnected with the police force. Merely a beneficiary of your father's Will who is to spend the night at Monument House.

Dora (*startled*) Here? But that's *impossible.* No-one *ever* spends the night here. Not if they *know* us.

Penworthy I'm sorry, Miss Dora. But it's a condition of your late father's and quite binding. He was most definite about it.

Lucien This is *intolerable.* Absolute *blackmail.*

Dora (*her eyes sparkling*) Oh, but Lucien—we can put her in the bedroom with the four-poster. I've always wanted to see how it worked with a *real* body in it.

Penworthy (*coughing*) I—er—I'm afraid *not,* Miss Dora. Not this time. The unexpected disappearance of Miss Ash might prove somewhat embarassing for all of us. She *is* rather famous, you see. I regret she'll have to leave here *alive.*

Dora (*put out*) That's so *typical* of Father. No consideration for any of us. How dare he force us to have this woman in our home? What right has he? What *right* has he, I say?

The bookcase secret door pivots open to reveal Emily Tomb. She is forty-six years old, and like her brother, distinctly overweight. She wears men's clothing, and has close-cropped hair. In the outside world she could easily be mistaken for an all-in wrestler. She is chewing an apple

Emily (*munching*) About five million poundsworth of right, at a rough guess. Wouldn't you say so, Penworthy?

Penworthy Good evening, Miss Emily.

Emily moves forward and the panel closes

Emily (*glancing at them all*) Vultures begining to gather, I see. All eager for their share of the carcass.

Dora (*frostily*) There's nothing of the vulture about me, Emily Tomb. Nothing at all.

Emily I'm sorry. Perhaps I should have referred to *you* as a carrion crow. After all—I notice you're trying to dress the part. (*She takes a bite of apple*)

Dora (*stung*) How dare you? How *dare* you!

Penworthy If you'll pardon my saying so, Miss Emily. This ridiculous enmity between you and your sister would be far better hidden whilst outsiders are present.

Emily *Ridiculous* enmity? (*She glares at Dora*) That old cow poisoned our mother.

Penworthy Mistakes happen with the most organized people, Miss Emily.

Though I myself would not have considered hemlock or foxgloves suitable ingredients for Flower Wine, obviously Miss Dora thought otherwise. And Mrs Tomb *did* compliment her on the taste before the convulsions began.

Emily (*sourly*) And I suppose that makes everything all right again, does it? Well nobody asked for your opinion, and just in passing, *I'll* decide the way I'm going to behave around here.

Penworthy That is, of course, entirely up to you. But if I might be permitted to quote from your late father's letter of instructions— (*He produces a letter from his inside pocket and opens it*) "And if that big-mouthed bitch Emily opens her trap in front of my guest, then she loses her share of the cash and you can split it between the rest of the morons..."

All react

Emily (*snarling*) Let *me* see that. (*She lumbers down to him and grabs the letter. She scans it rapidly, then blazes*) He can't *do* this!

Penworthy Nonetheless, he *has* done, Miss Emily, so I think it will be in your own interests to restrain yourself whilst Miss Ash is on the premises. Don't you agree?

Emily glares at him, then thrusts the letter back at him as he holds out his hand for it. She moves back to the fireplace

I need hardly add that Mr Tomb included similar instructions regarding the other members of the family. He—er—didn't want anyone to feel—left out, so to speak.

Lucien (*disbelievingly*) You mean he threatens *me* in that letter? *Me.*

Dora (*agitatedly*) There must be some mistake.

Penworthy (*gently*) There's no mistake, Miss Dora. Your father was most explicit. You are required to abstain from any mention of your—er—*horticultural* studies, and Mr Lucien his experiments in the East Wing.

Lucien This is monstrous. I refuse to be silenced. Absolutely refuse.

Dora But I don't understand, Mr Penworthy. What possible objection could there be to my mentioning our lovely gardens?

Emily (*growling*) Somebody might ask what you've *planted* in them.

Dora (*turning to her, peeved*) And why shouldn't they? Those beds are beautifully laid out.

Emily So are the bodies under them.

Lucien (*snapping*) You've been told about mentioning that before, Emily. It's a subject best left dead and buried.

Emily (*amused*) *You* said it. (*She bites into her apple*)

Dora (*to Penworthy*) But he's *never* said I mustn't talk about the gardens to our guests before. Never.

Emily That's because we haven't had guests before. At least—ones who had to be allowed to go home again.

Lucien (*firmly*) That is enough, Emily. I don't want to hear another word.

Emily (*glowering*) In that case, brother *dear*, you'd better stuff those piggy ears of yours with cotton-wool, because I haven't finished yet. Not by a long way. (*To Penworthy*) It doesn't take a great deal of imagination to work out what's behind all this, does it?

Penworthy All *what*, Miss Emily?

Emily These conditions. Threats. Whatever you want to call them. I think we all know why the old goat gave you that letter, don't we?

Lucien Well *I* certainly don't. I fail to see the reason entirely.

Dora So do I.

Emily (*with contempt*) Then you're even more stupid than I gave you credit for.

Lucien (*indignantly*) Well, really (*He moves away in pique*)

Emily (*her voice rising*) It's obvious, isn't it? All those little trips to London. The letters marked "Strictly private and personal". It's staring you in the face and you're too blind to see it.

As Emily is speaking, Marcus Tomb enters. He is forty-three years old and imagines himself to be Caesar. He wears a flowing white toga, purple lined and edged in gold, and a laurel crown. His feet are bare and sandalled

Marcus (*grandly*) What sayest thou to me now? Speak once again.

Emily (*glancing at him*) Keep out of this, peabrain, and get back to your nursemaid.

Penworthy Good evening, Mr Marcus.

Marcus (*recognizing him*) Why have you stol'n upon us thus? You, like Caesar's sister; the wife of Antony, should have an army for an usher, and the neighs of horses to tell of her approach long ere she did appear... (*He embraces Penworthy heartily*)

Lucien (*distastefully*) If you wouldn't *mind*. Marcus.

Marcus releases Penworthy and turns

We were just discussing a letter that Father gave to Mr Penworthy. A disgraceful document. Absolutely disgraceful.

Dora (*nodding eagerly*) Simply wicked, my dear.

Marcus (*suddenly pointing at the portrait*) Your letter did withold our breaking forth, till we perceiv'd both how you were wrong led and we in negligent danger.

Penworthy (*frowning*) Pardon?

Emily The scheming old devil. He's made fools of us all. Every single one of us.

Lucien (*tartly*) No-one's made a fool of *me*.

Emily They didn't *have* to. Nature did a first-class job. (*She snarls*) You fat imbecile. You haven't even the brains to understand what he *has* done. *I'm* the only one in this crackpot family who knows why we're all expected to act normal whilst his precious lady novelist is caged up with us.

Dora (*indignantly*) I will not stay here and be called a crackpot in my own home.

Lucien *My* home, dear. *My* home. I'm the eldest. (*To Emily*) But I quite agree with Dora. We refuse to be subjected to your unpleasant insinuations any longer. (*To Penworthy*) You may call us when the rest of the legatees are assembled.

Emily (*flopping into the wing-chair with a harsh laugh*) You see? You can't even face the truth.

Lucien (*purple with rage*) What truth?

Anne Franklin enters. She is a pretty girl of twenty-five to thirty wearing a nurse's uniform, and carrying a kidney-shaped steel dish which contains a hypodermic syringe and cotton-wool swabs. She moves towards Marcus

Emily (*loudly*) About *them*, you moronic monster. They're secretly married.

Everyone reacts in shock. Anne half turns and drops the dish

Lucien (*gaping*) Married?

Dora (*with her hand to her throat*) But they can't be. It's impossible.

Marcus (*gravely*) The people know it; and have receiv'd his accusations. (*His head drops on to his chest.*)

Emily (*triumphantly*) I thought that'd shake you. It's the only way it makes sense. He doesn't want his little bride to know she married into a family of lunatics.

Anne stoops and quickly gathers up her things

Lucien (*blazing*) Emily . . .

Emily (*heaving herself upright*) Face up to it, Lucy-boy. You're not trying to pretend we're just an average, home-loving family who spend our time doing good works for the community, are you? There's not one of us left this crumbling ruin for the past twenty years.

Dora (*fiercely*) There's never been the need. Everything we've ever wanted has been right here. The Chapel, the sick-room, the gardens *and* the burial grounds.

Emily (*sneering*) Oh, yes. We mustn't forget the burial grounds, must we? Even though we get more use out of the flower beds.

Lucien (*shouting*) Emily!

Emily (*standing*) Stop kidding yourselves. We haven't kept out of sight because we've wanted to. We've *had* to. We're the local Frankensteins. There's Oliver—chained up in the cellars thinking he's a werewolf . . .

A long howl comes from Oliver. Emily speaks through it

Marcus—so convinced he's Caesar, we expect him to be assassinated at any moment. Dotty Dora there—brewing up poisoned wines and popping off victims like ninepins—

Dora (*wailing*) Stop her, someone! Stop her!

Emily —and you. Fat little Lucien—locked in the East Wing mixing up your stinking chemicals and killing off half the wild life in the district!

Lucien (*puce with rage*) That is a lie! A dirty filthy lie!

Emily (*shouting him down*) Of course it is! (*She sneers*) And sweet little sister Monica is the Mother Superior of the local Convent, isn't she?

Dora (*trembling with agitation*) And what about *you*? You with your disgusting—depraved . . .! (*She flounders for words*)

Anne (*firmly*) Excuse me. (*She moves towards the door*)

Emily Oh, don't go, Nurse. I'm sure you'll not hear anything you don't already know.

Anne (*coldly*) I'm sure I won't, Miss Emily. But I have to change the needle and swabs. They're no longer sterile.

Emily I shouldn't let that worry you, dear. He'll be just as mad, no matter *what* you use on him.

Anne (*icily polite*) Mr Marcus is not mad, Miss Emily. Merely "disturbed". And he's been a lot better since we began treatment. Dr Fell has every confidence in its eventual success.

Emily (*sneering*) That charlatan. What does *he* know?

Anne Dr Fell is an *excellent* physician. Known and respected all over England. I think *you* might do worse than pay him a visit yourself.

Anne sweeps out of the room

Emily (*yelling after her*) Snotty little bitch! (*To the others*) And the sooner we get rid of *her*, the better. (*She glares at Marcus*) That goes for you too, bird-brain. Move!

Marcus (*his eyes narrowing*) No, Caesar shall not; danger knows full well that Caesar is more dangerous than he. We are two lions litter'd in one day, and I the elder and more terrible——

Lucien Oh, shut up, Marcus. No-one's going anywhere. *I* am head of this household, and Nurse Franklin will remain here until I see fit to dismiss her. Is that clear, Emily?

Penworthy gives a discreet cough

Penworthy If I might be allowed to put in a word? I'd just like to remind you that our guests should be arriving at any moment. It would be as wise to settle your differences before they do so.

Lucien Guests?

Emily (*glowering*) Did you say *guests*?

Dora (*alarmed*) More of them? You mean there are more?

Penworthy There's no cause for alarm, I assure you. The other person will not be remaining. He is merely a travelling companion of Miss Ash, and will be returning to London on the next train.

Lucien He? A man?

Dora (*horrified*) A *police* man?

Penworthy Miss Ash's *secretary*. Peregrine Potter, by name. (*To Dora*) So you see—there's nothing to be afraid of, is there?

Marcus (*clapping Dora's shoulder heartily*) Cowards die many times before their deaths; the valiant never taste of death but once.

Dora (*unsurely*) And he doesn't know about the Avon lady?

Lucien Of course he doesn't, Dora. How could he?

Dora Or the insurance salesman?

Penworthy Nothing at all, I promise you. However—to ensure that he *remains* in ignorance, it would be better if you refrained from offering him a sample of your home-made wine. Don't you agree?

Lucien (*pouring himself a drink from the same decanter that Penworthy used*) I consider that remark quite uncalled for, Penworthy. Dora may have her faults, but she'd never offer wine to a *servant*. It would be an obvious breach of social manners.

Emily I wouldn't let that worry you. He'd never live to tell.

Penworthy To be quite certain, though, I think Miss Dora's special brews had better be placed under lock and key until both our visitors have left. As I remarked earlier—accidents can happen (*He gives a dry laugh*)

Dora (*nodding*) I'll do it at once, shall I? Right away.

Lucien And *I*'ll hold the key.

Dora scuttles to the door, stops, turns, runs back to the drinks table, picks up the decanter both men used, plus one other, and turns to exit again

Dora (*with a sheepish giggle*) I almost forgot *these*.

Penworthy and Lucien react

Penworthy (*with difficulty*) Miss Dora . . .

Dora (*about to exit*) Yes?

Penworthy (*indicating the decanter*) One of yours??

Dora (*all smiles*) Why, yes. It's my Mock-Crusted Port. (*She realizes*) Did you like it?

Penworthy's hand goes to his throat. Lucien's glass falls from his nerveless fingers.

Lucien (*hoarsely*) Nurse . . . (*louder*) Nurse . . .!

Dora (*startled*) What is it, Lucien? (*She looks at the glass on the floor*) Oh—*you* drank some, too. (*She gives a sudden light laugh*) It's all right, silly. It's perfectly safe. I made it from plums. (*She lifts the other decanter*) *This* is the one that's poisonous.

Giggling happily, Dora exits

Penworthy and Lucien look sheepish. Emily gives a bellow of laughter

Anne enters with a fresh syringe and swabs in the dish

Anne (*as she enters*) Did you call, Mr Lucien? (*She moves to Marcus*)

Lucien No. No. It was nothing. (*He coughs and turns away*)

Anne (*to Marcus*) Let me have your arm, Marcus.

Emily (*snarling*) You're not going to stick that thing into him now, are you? Not while we're here?

Anne That was the idea, Miss Emily. Hardly a novel sight for you after all this time. (*She prepares the needle*)

Marcus solemnly exposes his upper arm

Penworthy Er—Nurse . . .

Anne (*turning*) Yes, Mr Penworthy?

Penworthy Would you help Mr Marcus change into something—er—a little less *noticeable* for the Will reading? The late Mr Tomb requested that it be a slightly more formal gathering as outsiders will be present.

Anne (*surprised*) Outsiders? Here? (*Recovering*) I—er—I'm sorry. I didn't mean to . . . Yes. Yes, of course. (*To Marcus*) Come along, Marcus. I—er—I'll do this upstairs. Let's get you out of your toga and into a nice suit, shall we? (*She takes his arm and collects the steel dish, etc.*)

Marcus I thank you for your pains and courtesy.

Anne and Marcus exit

Emily (*looking after them*) Whey-faced little trollop. (*To Penworthy*) The old man hasn't left *her* anything, has he?

Penworthy Just a small legacy, Miss Emily.

Emily *How* small?

Penworthy A token sum for faithful service over the past two years. Nothing untoward, I assure you.

Emily You don't assure me at all, you old crook. There's something fishy going on around here, and I want to know what it is. Is this Ash woman married to the old man or isn't she? Come on. Out with it. If anybody knows, it's you.

Penworthy To the best of my knowledge, Miss Ash and your father have never even met. More than that, I am unable to tell you at the moment.

Lucien And what's that supposed to mean?

Emily (*taking Penworthy by the lapels*) It's been six weeks now since the late unlamented passed on, and we still don't know how much cash is coming to us. (*She begins to shake him slowly*) I'm warning you, Penworthy. If you're up to something, I'm going to snap you into little pieces and plant you with Dora's mistakes. Understand?

Penworthy (*choking*) My dear Miss Emily. I am a highly respectable solicitor.

Emily If you were respectable, you wouldn't be working for this family. (*She gives him a final shake and releases him*)

Lucien (*outraged*) Really, Emily.

Penworthy (*tidying himself*) Naturally I understand your impatience at the delay, but my instructions were quite explicit. There have been a great many details to attend to, and vast wealth does create certain problems, you know.

Emily So does the lack of it. I need that money. Fast.

Lucien So do I. My experiments have come to a complete halt due to my financial difficulties. Further delays may cause complete disaster, and I'm sure the Prime Minister would be very annoyed if *that* happened.

Penworthy I promise you'll get everything that's coming to you within twenty-four hours. Word of honour.

Agatha Hammond enters. Housekeeper to the family for over forty years, she is grim, outspoken and unlovely. She is aged about sixty-five, sallow faced, and her hair is scraped back into an untidy bun. She is dressed in unrelieved black

Agatha (*flatly*) There's a phone call. For him. (*She indicates Penworthy with a tilt of her head*) Say's it's urgent.

Lucien Who is it, Agatha?

Agatha Him from the car hire down the village.

Penworthy Ah, yes. Draycott. He's collecting our guests from the station. (*He moves towards the door*)

Agatha He'll find that difficult. They've not arrived.
Penworthy (*startled*) Not . . . (*He recovers*) I'd better speak to him.

Penworthy hurries out

Lucien (*fuming*) I knew it. I *knew* it. More delays. (*To Agatha*) He's sure he hasn't just missed them I suppose?
Agatha He could hardly do that, Mr Lucien. The train didn't stop. Went through without so much as a whistle. I suppose this means we'll be eating as normal? We'll not be wanting the extra place?
Lucien Never mind the extra place. What about the *Will reading*?
Emily We'll have that as soon as Penworthy gets off the telephone.
Lucien (*irately*) How can we? He's already told us he can't read it until everyone is here. (*Loudly*) I am *most* annoyed.
Emily Keep your shirt on, Lucy-boy. He'll read it.
Agatha Lot of fuss about nothing, if you ask me. Wills are meant to be read when people are dead. Not when they're playing hide-and-seek. (*She moves to the door*)
Lucien (*warningly*) Agatha.
Agatha (*turning*) Your father is about as dead as I am, Mr Lucien. I heard what I heard, and I know what I know, and that's enough for me.
Emily (*snarling*) And it's enough for *me* to know I saw the old maniac sealed in that mausoleum six weeks ago with a marble slab over his ugly face. Understand?
Agatha (*still flatly*) You saw his coffin interred, Miss Emily. I'll grant you that. (*Darkly*) But which of you actually *saw* him inside it? (*Fiercely*) *None* of you. That box was screwed down and sealed before they'd let anyone into the room. Isn't that true?
Emily What did you expect? They didn't want us to catch whatever it was he died of. The quack told us it was highly infectious.
Agatha (*Nodding grimly*) And you all believed him? (*Fiercely*) Doctors have been bribed before today. He's not dead. Not him. I've heard him moving about the house. Down in the cellars and in the passages. I've heard him here—in this very room—night after night.
Emily You've been hitting the cooking sherry again, you old bat.
Agatha (*shaking her head*) I'd recognize that voice of his *anywhere. And* the other one.
Lucien Who was it?
Agatha (*shaking her head again*) That's his business, not mine. I'm only a servant in this house. When he wants you to know what's going on, he'll tell you himself—just like he always has done.
Emily Can't you get it into your thick skull, he's dead? Dead.
Agatha (*glancing at her*) Your father is a strange man, Miss Emily. If he wants everyone to think he's dead, then he must have good reason. I've questioned nothing he's done or said these last forty years, so I'll play along with his little games now; but I'd sincerely advise you all to watch your tongues for the next few days. Now if you'll excuse me, I'll go and see to the meal.

Agatha exits

Emily (*looking after her*) She's mad. Stark, staring mad.
Lucien (*uneasily*) But what if she's right? If he isn't dead?
Emily (*harshly*) Of course he's dead, you brainless toad. Dead and rotting by this time. She's trying to put the wind up us, that's all.
Lucien But why?
Emily I'm trying to think. (*Her eyes narrow*) Got it. (*She snaps her fingers*) Penworthy. *He*'s the brains behind this one.
Lucien Penworthy?
Emily Of course. (*She moves to the drinks table*) Hamilton-clever-Penworthy. Our respectable family solicitor. If you'll use that feeble little brain of yours for a few minutes, you'll see I'm right. Who's in the best position to try and swindle us out of our money? Penworthy. Who's kept us waiting six weeks before finally making up his mind to let us know what's in the old man's Will? Penworthy. And who's the only one who knows anything about this mysterious Ash woman? *Penworthy.*
Lucien (*after a moment*) What are we going to do?
Emily (*lowering herself into the wing-chair*) I'll tell you . . .

There is a loud knocking at the outer door. Emily and Lucien look at each other, startled

Lucien (*almost in a whisper*) Them?
Emily (*half rising*) Can't be. The train went straight through.

There is a moment's silence

Lucien Shall I answer it?
Emily No. Leave it to Agatha. That's what she's paid for, isn't it?

The sound of heavy bolts being drawn is heard. The hinges groan loudly as the door is opened

Freda (*off*) Oh, Good evening. This *is* Monument House, isn't it? The residence of the Tomb family? Oh, thank goodness for that. I thought we were lost. The fog, you know. I believe you're expecting me. Ash is the name. Ermyntrude Ash.
Lucien It *is* her.

Lucien and Emily hurry to the door to peer

Agatha (*off*) You'd best come in, I suppose. I'll tell them you're here.
Perry (*off*) Thank you.

The sound of the door closing is heard

Agatha (*off*) Through there.

Emily and Lucien almost fall over each other in their hurry to get back into the room

Freda Mountjoy and Peregrine (Perry) Potter enter, followed by Agatha. Freda is a smart, slim, middle-aged woman, wearing a jaunty hat and coat over a smart two-piece suit. Perry is a nervous thirty-five-year-old, looking most uncomfortable in a dark suit and white shirt

The Ash woman and friend.

Freda's eyebrows lift

I'll tell Mr Penworthy they've arrived.

Agatha exits

Emily (*eyeing Freda*) So . . . You're the mysterious Miss Ash, are you?
Freda Er—yes. (*Trying to be friendly*) Good evening, Miss . . .?
Emily Tomb. Emily Tomb. And this is my brother, Lucien.
Lucien The famous scientist.
Freda (*indicating Perry*) My—er—my secretary, Mr Potter.
Perry (*extending his hand to Emily*) How do you do?
Emily (*ignoring it*) We expected you to come by train, Miss Ash.
Lucien Even sent a taxi to the station for you.
Freda I'm terribly sorry, but we *had* to come down by car. It seems that the train doesn't stop at your local station on Saturdays during winter, and what with the fog warning on the radio this afternoon, we thought it best to set off as soon as possible. We did try to warn you, but your number is ex-directory. I do hope we haven't kept you waiting too long?
Emily We've been waiting six weeks, so I suppose we can last out another few minutes. (*She turns away*) Drink?
Freda (*removing her topcoat*) Thank you. A small sherry if you have it. (*She puts the coat on the writing-table*)
Perry Not for me, thanks. I don't drink.
Lucien (*offering a cigarette-box*) Smoke?
Perry I don't smoke, either.
Emily (*pouring the drinks*) Really? I do hope you're not going to tell us you make your own *dresses*. (*Taking a glass to Freda*) One sherry coming up.
Lucien (*looking pointedly at the glass*) Emily . . .
Emily Relax. It's a good one.
Freda (*taking the glass*) Thank you. (*She smiles*) To tell you the truth, I couldn't tell a good one from a cheap one.
Emily You would if it were one of Dora's.
Lucien That's our sister. She makes wine as a hobby.
Freda How very interesting. And are they always successful?
Emily No-one's ever complained. (*She moves up to the fire and puts another log on*)
Freda (*sipping*) I suppose she gets most of her ingredients from the gardens? You must have simply *acres* of them, if the drive is anything to go by. (*Brightly*) I love gardening, don't you? It's so *relaxing*—puts you at peace with the world. (*She smiles*) Give me half a chance to get into those rose beds of yours, and I'd never come out again.
Emily (*drily*) Not without an exhumation order, and that's for sure.

Before any further development can take place, Penworthy hurries into the room

Penworthy My dear Miss Ash. (*He wrings her hand*) Welcome to Monument

House. (*He realizes*) Forgive me. Hamilton Penworthy, the family solicitor. I—er—I see you've already met Miss Emily and Mr Lucien. The others will be right down. (*He indicates a chair*) Please be seated.

Freda Thank you, but I'd prefer to stand for the moment. It's been a long drive. Visibility was very poor. Perry had an awful job getting us here. I don't drive myself, you see. (*She indicates Perry*) My secretary, Peregrine Potter.

Perry (*extending his hand*) Hello.

Penworthy (*Ignoring him*) How very kind of you to spare the time to come down here. I realize, of course, how busy you must be . . .

Freda Well—I *am* in the middle of my new book, *Daughter of Allah*, but I just couldn't resist it. I mean—it's like something out of one of my own stories. Being left a legacy by a perfect stranger. Simply fantastic.

Perry I'll say.

Penworthy There was nothing perfect about the late Mr Tomb, I'm afraid. He was a man of *many* vices. However, your books made him very happy. I understand that in his own room he had copies of every book you'd ever written, so obviously they made a great impression on him. A very great impression.

Emily Especially when the bookcase collapsed and he finished up underneath them all.

Perry gives a nervous laugh, then chokes it

Lucien (*glaring at him*) It wasn't funny at the time. He contracted some rare disease from the woodwork and died shortly afterwards—so we're told.

Penworthy But not before he made over a portion of his estate to you in gratitude for what you'd done for him. The late Mr Tomb was a very rich man, and I'm sure you'll be more than pleased with what he left you.

Freda I'm sure I shall. I mean—I never expected . . .

Emily Neither did we. But now that you do, I'm sure you wouldn't mind if the rest of us found out exactly what *we've* got coming to us. (*To Penworthy*) Penworthy.

Penworthy Er—yes. I see no further reason for delay. (*He goes to the internal telephone and picks it up*) I'll ask Mrs Hammond to summon the rest of the family.

Emily Don't bother. I'll go find Monica, and Lucien can get the others.

Lucien Good idea. (*To Freda*) Excuse me.

Lucien exits

Penworthy (*replacing the telephone*) I'm not sure where you'll find Miss Monica. I haven't seen her all day.

Emily Don't worry. I've got an infallible system for tracking that one down. It never fails.

Penworthy What's that?

Emily I just whisper that there's a man in the house, and there she is.

Emily exits

Penworthy (*giving an embarrassed cough*) Always joking, our Miss Emily. (*He gives a little laugh*)

Freda Yes. (*She glances at Perry*)

Perry Yes.

Freda (*after a slight pause*) I hope you'll forgive me if I'm mistaken, Mr Penworthy—but I rather feel that I'm not exactly a *welcome* guest here.

Penworthy (*aghast*) My dear Miss Ash . . .

Freda (*quickly*) No, no, it's quite all right. I understand perfectly. It's only natural for them to resent my presence under the circumstances. From their point of view I've no right to be here at all. They don't know *me*, and I don't know *them*. Why the late Mr Tomb wanted to make *me* a beneficiary I can't imagine. (*Curiously*) How much am I supposed to inherit from the estate, as a matter of interest?

Penworthy Like the others, I'm afraid you'll have to wait until the reading to find that out. I'm sorry, but I can make no exceptions.

Freda (*ruefully*) I was afraid you'd say that, only it's so foggy outside, and rather a long drive back to London. If you could have told me quietly, I'd have left without more ado. I have no wish to upset the family, and in any case intend to give the money to a suitable charity.

Penworthy (*spluttering*) Charity? (*Choking*) Excuse me. (*He coughs wildly*) I've just remembered something. Something important.

Penworthy staggers to the door and exits

For a moment they stare after him, then Freda throws a quick glance at Perry, moves to the doors and quietly closes them. Keeping her back to the doors, she speaks to him

Freda And what did you make of all *that*?

Perry (*uncertainly*) Well—it certainly *seemed* to work.

Freda Oh, Perry. Of course it worked. It always does. They don't suspect a thing.

Perry I suppose not. But . . . (*He stops helplessly*)

Freda But what? (*She moves to him*)

Perry You're sure we'll get away with it? I mean—we've never pulled anything like *this* before, have we? This time we're dealing with the Law.

Freda (*patting his cheek*) And do you think I've never dealt with the Law before, darling? Being the widow of a High Court Judge *has* its advantages. (*Seriously*) Now listen. By the look of things, we're not going to find out much until the whole family's gathered together, but with a bit of luck we'll know exactly how much the mythical Miss Ash is inheriting within the next hour. Agreed?

Perry (*nodding*) Agreed. But I'd hardly call her the *mythical* Miss Ash. I mean—after all—she has written quite a few books, you know.

Freda True. But we both know that very few people have actually met her, don't we? In fact, you can count them on one hand, so there's no chance of being recognized and accused of impersonation, is there? Now, let's assume we've got the Will reading over with and know where we stand. What do you do then?

Perry I—er—I excuse myself, explaining I have to go back to London. Get into the car, make for the rendezvous, then wait for your call. Right?

Freda Right. Now don't worry. Everything's going to be fine.

Perry I wish I were as confident as you, Freda.

Freda (*laughing*) Well you know what they say about me? The biggest little con-merchant in the game. That's how I've managed to get away with it so long. The difference a few clothes and a new hair-style makes. (*Seriously*) Now, according to this Penworthy character, I'm supposed to stay here overnight—which is a bit of a bore. However, I'll get away first thing tomorrow morning and I should be with you no later than half-past eight at a rough guess, so don't forget to meet me.

Perry I'll be there. Shaking like a leaf.

Freda It's going to be a walk-over. I can feel it.

Perry If you say so. (*He looks round*) Is that the late lamented, do you think?

Freda Looks more like Dracula's grandfather to me. It's enough to give you the willies. But it's this *room* that interests me.

Perry (*puzzled*) Why?

Freda Haven't you noticed anything—odd?

Perry (*helplessly*) Like what?

Freda The bookcases, for instance. They're all empty. In fact, apart from that one over there—(*She indicates the Bible on the table*)—there isn't a book in the room.

Perry Oh, *that*. Yes, well . . .

Freda (*moving around*) Here we are—in a multi-millionaire's library, and there isn't a single book on the shelves. Now in view of what we've been told, doesn't that strike you as being a little *strange*?

Perry Well . . .

Freda (*turning*) If you ask me, Septimus Tomb never read a book in his life.

Perry But he must have done. Or else . . .

Freda Why leave Ermyntrude Ash what may turn out to be a small fortune in his Will? Exactly.

Perry (*bewildered*) The whole thing sounds crazy to me.

Freda By the look of that painting, and the two bright sparks we met earlier, *I'm* beginning to think that the whole family may be only sixty pence to the pound. We're going to have to move very carefully, Perry. Very carefully indeed.

The wolf howl sounds

Perry (*frowning*) Didn't notice any dogs when we arrived, did you? (*He laughs nervously*) Sounded almost like a wolf.

Lucien (*off*) Quiet, down there!

Freda They're coming back. Now remember. Relax and leave everything to me.

The doors open and Penworthy enters, followed by Dora, Lucien, Marcus, now in a suit, and Anne. Agatha follows up the rear and closes the doors

Penworthy Forgive me, Miss Ash. A slight lapse of memory on my part, but all is settled now. May I introduce you to the others? Miss Dora Tomb and Mr Marcus Tomb. (*He indicates them*)

Freda (*warmly*) How do you do?

They stare at her in silence

Penworthy Miss Franklin, our resident nurse.

Anne (*smiling*) Hello.

Penworthy And Mrs Hammond, the housekeeper whom you have already met, of course. (*To the others*) Miss Ermyntrude Ash, the famous novelist.

Freda (*indicating Perry*) And this is Perry—my faithful secretary.

Perry (*advancing to Dora, with his hand outstretched*) Hello.

Dora (*recoiling with a shriek*) No.

Perry stops and looks at his hand in surprise

Anne (*edging Marcus forward*) Marcus. Shake hands with Mr Perry.

Marcus (*drawing back*) Let me have men about me that are fat; sleek-headed men, and such as sleep o' nights. Yon Cassius has a lean and hungry look. He thinks too much: such men are dangerous.

Freda's eyebrows rise and she looks at Anne

Anne (*quickly*) Very good, Marcus. That was word perfect. (*To Freda and Perry*) He's studying the role of Caesar for the Town Festival, you know.

Freda How—interesting.

Anne (*smiling*) Isn't it? (*To Marcus*) Perhaps we'd better sit down, had we? (*She takes his arm*)

Penworthy A good idea. Miss Monica and Miss Emily will be with us shortly so if you wouldn't mind . . . (*He indicates the chairs*)

Everyone moves to the chairs. Dora keeping a nervous eye on Perry. Penworthy takes up the deeds box and begins to sort through it. Seating is as follows: front row downstage: empty, empty, Dora, Lucien. Back row downstage: Freda, Agatha, Anne, Marcus. Perry is left standing, so takes a chair from the front row and puts it beside Freda. He is about to sit when voices are heard, off

Monica (*off*) Take your hands off me, you fat bitch!

Emily (*off*) In there, tramp!

The doors fly open and Monica Tomb is propelled into the room, followed by Emily. Monica is an extremely attractive woman of thirty-five, with a stunning figure. She wears a skin-tight gown, low cut, and her hair cascades about her shoulders

Penworthy (*turning*) Ah, Miss Monica.

Monica (*ignoring him and turning to Emily*) Lay those flabby fingers of yours on me again, sister dear, and I'll bite them off at the elbows. Understand?

Penworthy (*firmly*) Miss Monica. We have guests present.

Monica (*snarling*) Tell them to get knotted. And you can . . . (*She sees Perry*) Oh. (*She smoothes herself down quickly*)

Penworthy May I introduce you to Miss Ermyntrude Ash, the novelist, and Mr Potter, her secretary.
Perry *Peregrine* Potter, that is. (*He moves forward and holds his hand out to her*)
Monica (*taking it eagerly*) Hello. (*She mouths a kiss at him*)

Startled, Perry tries to withdraw his hand, but Monica refuses to let go. With a great deal of effort he manages to free himself and totters backwards to his chair

Emily (*lumbering to the chair beside Dora*) Calm down, hot-lips. Dinner isn't till *after* the reading. (*She sits*)
Monica (*sweetly*) In that case, we'll have plenty of time to bring your trough through here, won't we? (*She blows another kiss at Perry*)
Freda (*clearing her throat*) Good evening, Miss Tomb. (*She half rises*)
Monica (*looking her over*) Hmm. So you're the mysterious Emmy Ash, are you? No wonder the Old Man took such a shine to you. You're quite a dish for an old lady.
Freda (*taken aback*) Well—thank you.
Monica (*oozing over to stand beside Perry*) I've read a couple of your books, as a matter of fact. (*She toys with Perry's hair, to his obvious discomfort*)
Freda Oh. And—did you like them?
Monica No. (*She moves behind Perry, and plays with his tie*)
Freda I see.
Monica (*sliding her fingers inside Perry's shirt*) No offence, but all that romantic slush doesn't do a thing for me. I prefer the *real* thing. Hot and *strong*.

Perry gives a gasp as she squeezes him under his shirt

Penworthy Ahem.
Monica (*removing her hand from Perry's chest*) Looks like the fun's going to start. I'd better make myself comfortable. (*With a wriggle, she moves down to the wing-chair and settles herself in*) I can hear *perfectly* from here, Mr Penworthy. Take it away. The floor's yours. (*She pours herself a drink*)

Penworthy clears his throat, rustles his papers and moves behind the writing-table

Penworthy (*surveying them*) First of all I'd like to thank you all for being here this evening.
Emily This is a Will reading, not a garden party. Get on with it.
Penworthy As you all know, Mr Tomb was one of the country's richest men, and is now . . .
Emily One of the deadest. Skip the lecture and get on to how much he left and what we're getting out of it.
Penworthy (*annoyed*) If I might be allowed to *continue*, Miss Emily?

Emily glowers but is silent

Thank you. (*Pause*) Shortly before his death, instructions were issued to convert all his assets, with the exception of this house and its grounds, into cash. This was done—much against my advice, I might add, and realized the total of seven million pounds.

An excited rustle fills the room

Emily How much of it's mine?
Penworthy (*ignoring her*) Of this seven million pounds handed over to him, three million was deposited in a London bank, and the rest was retained by Mr Tomb himself. Unfortunately, we have no idea what he did with it.
Lucien (*rising*) You mean—it's vanished? Four million pounds?
Penworthy Exactly. Gone without trace. (*He holds up his hands as the babble begins*) However, whilst the search for it goes on, I am required to read to you the contents of his Last Will and Testament, and the conditions therein. (*He sits and waits for them all to quieten*) To begin with—Mr Tomb insisted on writing out his own Will, scorning my advice and experience. It was delivered to me with a covering letter concerning certain instructions which I have carried out, and now I am ready to reveal its contents. (*He opens the Will*)
Emily And not before time.
Lucien Do be quiet, Emily.
Penworthy (*reading*) "To each of my six children: Lucien, Emily, Marcus, Dora Lucrezia, Monica and Oliver, the sum of four hundred thousand pounds each.

There is general reaction

To my housekeeper, Agatha Hammond, and my son's nurse, Anne Elisabeth Franklin, providing they are still in my service at the time of my death, the sum of one hundred thousand pounds each.

There is general reaction

To my solicitor, Hamilton Penworthy, the sum of four hundred thousand pounds. (*Pause*) The remainder of my estate, I leave to Miss Ermyntrude Ash, a writer of romantic novels, residing at an unknown address, but I suspect in London. This I do in gratitude for what she's done for me."
Freda (*Baffled*) But I haven't . . .
Penworthy "As you all know, I've suffered with insomnia for many years, and her books put me to sleep quicker than any tablets that quack doctor ever gives me."

Perry gives a nervous laugh then chokes it

"If, however, she chooses not to accept this legacy, then split it between the rest of them in equal shares."
Dora (*jumping up*) Forgery. It's a forgery.
Emily We'll fight this through every court in the land.
Lucien (*spluttering*) Four million pounds. To an absolute stranger.
Monica Not forgetting the house.
Dora She can't possibly accept it. That money belongs to us. Every penny of it. It's ours. The family's.

Anne (*quietly rising and looking at Freda*) Congratulations, Miss Ash. I'm very happy for you.
Freda (*with a quick, tight smile*) Thank you.
Penworthy (*slightly louder*) There is a *further* passage . . .
Lucien Ah . . .

All look at Penworthy expectantly

Penworthy "In order to protect his interests, if Miss Ash decides to accept this legacy, she is required to take up residence in Monument House."
Freda (*stunned*) What?
Penworthy (*with a smile*) He wanted all your future novels to be written here.
Freda (*rising*) But I'm afraid that's out of the question, Mr Penworthy. I couldn't possibly stay in this house. Under any circumstances.
Penworthy Four million pounds, Miss Ash. It's a lot of money.
Perry (*dazed*) Four million.
Freda (*uncertainly*) I . . . (*She looks at Perry*) I can't think. (*She sits*)
Anne (*to Penworthy*) Excuse me. But as I've never been left anything in a Will before, I wonder if you can give me any idea of when I might get the money?
Emily The nightingale's showing her claws at last, I see.
Anne (*coldly*) I'm not asking for myself, Miss Emily. I have a very good reason for wanting to know.
Emily I'll bet.
Penworthy (*uncomfortably*) Ah—I regret to have to tell you this, Miss Franklin—but here we encounter a slight *setback*, so to speak.
Monica Setback?

All look at Penworthy

Penworthy (*most apologetically*) As I told you earlier, of the seven million realized, Mr Tomb himself took four. The—er—the missing millions which appear to be the property of Miss Ash at the moment.
Lucien Yes, yes. Go on.
Penworthy Unfortunately—in making his arrangements for the disposal of his wealth—he quite forgot about death duties.
Dora Death duties?
Monica What about them?
Penworthy Well, in this case—the death duties on the Tomb fortune amount to—three million pounds—

Everyone registers shock

—and as this was all the money we could find—it has been turned over to Her Majesty's Government as requested. There's not a penny left.
Lucien (*gaping*) You—you mean . . .
Emily (*rising*) We've got *nothing*?
Dora We're penniless?
Monica It's a fix! A carve-up!
Penworthy Unfortunately, we are all in the same boat. None of us will

receive a brass farthing unless the other four million is found and Miss Ash refuses her portion . . .

Lucien (*whirling to face Freda*) But she *has* refused, haven't you? You can't change your mind now.

Penworthy Miss Ash has until tomorrow morning. I cannot take an acceptance or refusal until that time. My hands are tied.

Emily And so will your throat be if she walks off with that money.

Dora (*to Penworthy*) You're a lawyer. Do something!

Penworthy (*spreading his hands*) I can do nothing until the appointed time. Now I suggest you all go to your rooms and prepare yourselves for dinner.

Emily Dinner?

Penworthy Miss Ash has a lot to think about. I think we should leave her in solitude for a short while.

Agatha (*finally rising*) It'll be twenty minutes. (*She looks Freda up and down grimly*) That should give her *plenty* of time.

Agatha exits

Anne (*helping Marcus up*) Come along, Marcus. Back to your room.

Marcus (*gravely*) Caesar shall forth; the things that threaten'd me ne'er look'd but on my back; when they shall see the face of Caesar they are vanished.

Anne (*glancing at Perry and Freda*) That's right. Perfect again. (*To them*) Excuse us. And don't worry. They can't do a thing about it. It's all yours.

Anne exits with Marcus. Lucien, Dora and Emily glare at Freda, then follow the others out

There is a silence

Penworthy Well, Miss Ash. You're a very fortunate lady.

Freda (*shakily*) So it would seem. (*She glances at Perry again*)

Penworthy It's a lot of money—if we find it.

Freda Yes.

Perry (*suddenly*) I—I wonder if you'll excuse me?

Freda (*alarmed*) Perry?

Perry I really should be getting back to London.

Monica You're not leaving? Not tonight?

Perry (*gulping*) I'm afraid I've got to. Work, you know.

Monica (*quickly*) But it's foggy outside. I'm sure I can find a warm bed for you here.

Perry It's most kind of you—but I'll really have to be going.

Freda Perry?

Perry (*to her*) Do what you think best. I—I'll leave it to you. See you tomorrow—at the office.

Freda (*uncertainly*) But . . . (*Taking a grip on herself*) Right. I'll see you first thing. Drive carefully.

Monica (*eagerly*) I'll see you to your car.

Perry exits hurriedly, chased by Monica

Penworthy moves to the doors and closes them

Penworthy You intend to work tomorrow as usual, Miss Ash? After all this excitement?

Freda (*shakily*) Nothing like work for keeping the mind active.

Penworthy How right you are, my dear. My own thought exactly. (*He moves to the drinks table and pours two drinks with his back to the audience*) A little toast to your new-found wealth—always providing you accept it, of course. (*He takes a glass to her*)

Freda (*accepting it*) I don't see how I can. I mean—I never expected I'd have to live here to inherit. It's just impossible.

Penworthy Then you intend to refuse?

Freda I didn't say that. I've still to think things over. I mean—it will have its advantages, of course . . . (*She sips*)

Penworthy But also its drawbacks. (*He sips his drink*)

Freda I'm afraid so. On the other hand—I *might* be able to work something out. Subject to certain conditions of my own. (*She moves to the fireplace*) Four million pounds.

Penworthy If we find it.

Freda (*turning*) But there *is* the house.

Penworthy As you say. There is the house.

Freda And four million pounds is a lot of money to have in cash, Mr Penworthy, isn't it? It would take up an awful lot of room, wouldn't you think?

Penworthy Well—yes.

Freda Then hasn't it crossed your mind that most probably it's here? Hidden away somewhere inside Monument House?

Penworthy I must admit that I too shared your notion, Miss Ash, but an extensive search has failed to reveal its whereabouts.

Freda Perhaps you haven't been searching in the right places. Maybe I can do better. (*She sips at her glass*)

Penworthy You mean . . .

Freda I've decided to accept. If there's four million pounds in this house, I'm going to have it. It's legally mine, and I know just what I'm going to do with it.

Penworthy But what about the family?

Freda Oh, I'll see them all right, don't worry. But they'll have to go. I can't have them hanging around while I'm—writing.

Penworthy So your mind is made up?

Freda (*with a smile*) Yes. it is. (*She moves to the wing-chair and sits*) Quite made up.

Penworthy (*drawing a deep breath*) Miss Ash—I will be quite honest with you. I had hoped that you might, under the circumstances, waive your rights to the house and fortune. After all, you did not know Mr Tomb, and he had never met you. Agreed?

Freda Agreed.

Penworthy I see now that this was a vain hope. You have every intention of claiming your inheritance.

Freda does not reply, but sits smiling, glass in her hand

This places me in rather an awkward position. (*He moves to the fireplace*) For many years I have handled the affairs of this family, and have been told several times that I would benefit greatly for my services under Mr Tomb's Will. No doubt the sum of four hundred thousand pounds would appear to you adequate reward, but I'm afraid I anticipated rather more, and acted accordingly.

Freda continues to smile, not flinching a muscle as Penworthy roams around the room

Over a period of time I incurred debts of over one million pounds. A sum that needs repaying rather urgently. You, Miss Ash, are the only person who can help me at this time, so therefore, I shall have the money from *you*.

Behind Penworthy, the secret door begins to open

Not all at once, you understand. One must be discreet. But little by little the money will flow to me, and soon I will have it all. (*He suddenly notices the open panel*) Excuse me. (*He moves to the opening and looks inside*) It's quite all right. Miss Ash and I have come to an agreement which will satisfy *all* parties—for the time being. (*He turns away and moves back to Freda*) So, you see—everything is going to plan. Just as I said it would. (*He rests his hand on Freda's shoulder*)

Without a flicker of emotion, she topples slowly on to the floor, stone dead. Penworthy smiles down at her as—

the CURTAIN *slowly falls*

ACT II

Scene 1

The same. Fifteen minutes later

The body of Freda has been removed and the secret panel is closed. Penworthy stands at the octagonal table, hand resting on the Bible, facing front. Dora, a rapt look on her face, is sitting on one of the dining-chairs, whilst Lucien, glass in hand, is standing by the fireplace, a scowl on his face. Emily sits perched on the table edge, munching an apple, and Monica stands behind the wing-chair. Penworthy is speaking

Penworthy . . . Naturally I summoned the aid of Nurse Franklin but it was too late. Miss Ash was beyond mortal help. (*Sadly*) It was her heart, of course. And the shock of the inheritance.

Lucien (*fuming*) That's all very well, Penworthy, but why did the wretched woman want to drop dead in *this* house? Couldn't she have had the decency to wait until she'd arrived home?

Penworthy My dear Mr Lucien——

Emily (*cutting in*) Well, you must admit it's very *opportune*. For everybody.

Penworthy But naturally. It would be hypocritical of us to pretend otherwise. We all stand to gain a great deal from this unfortunate event, do we not? Whereas before we had nothing, we now have the house to share between us.

Monica Not to mention four million pounds.

Lucien If we ever find them.

Penworthy Oh, we shall. Never fear. But to return to the subject of Miss Ash. She is—(*he coughs*)—I mean—*was* a well-known novelist. Her unexpected demise is bound to cause comment in the outside world. Comment, and perhaps even *suspicion.*

Lucien Suspicion?

Penworthy (*mildly*) But of course. Under the circumstances, an autopsy will be performed, and an inquest will be a matter of course. I need hardly add that *all* of us may be called to give evidence—especially if it turns out that she had no previous record of heart trouble.

Dora Oh. (*She looks at the others in anguish*)

Lucien (*spluttering*) Are you suggesting that because a perfect stranger chooses to have her heart attack in this house, the whole family is to be subjected to public investigation? I won't allow it. Do you hear, Penworthy. I won't allow it.

Emily (*heaving herself off the table*) I don't think we need worry about that, sweetie pie. There's quite a *simple* way of avoiding an investigation—isn't there, Penworthy?

All look at Penworthy

Penworthy (*with a gentle cough*) As Miss Emily suggests—we *do* have a way out of our difficulty.

Emily (*Taking a huge bite of apple and speaking with her mouth full*) Provided we keep our heads . . .

Lucien I *always* keep *my* head.

Emily (*glancing at him*) We can fix it so that nobody knows anything about what's happened.

Monica How?

Emily By putting them off the scent. Sending them on a wild goose chase.

Dora (*bewilderedly*) I don't understand. (*She looks at Lucien*)

Emily (*sweetly*) Of course you don't, little bird-brain. But Penworthy does. (*She looks at him*) Don't you?

Penworthy Miss Emily's solution to the problem is this, I think. No-one—I repeat—*no-one* has any need to know that Miss Ash died here—in this house. Her Secretary had already left the premises, and was well on his way to London when the incident occurred. That being the case, with the exception of us, there is no-one in a position to prove that she has not *followed* him.

Lucien (*pleased*) So there's no need to bring the police into this after all? Interfering busybodies. Let them chase motorists.

Dora (*beaming*) And we can put her under the rose-beds with the Morris Dancing team.

Lucien (*glowering at her*) Really, Dora. Sometimes I think you go *too* far.

Monica There's just one thing.

All look at Monica

What's going to happen when she doesn't show up in London? This is the first place they're going to look for her.

Penworthy Of course. But if we present them with *irrefutable* proof that Miss Ash returned to London . . . (*He spreads his hands*)

Monica And how do we do that?

Penworthy We have in our possession the lady's clothing. It being exceedingly foggy at the moment, I feel sure that a female figure attired in those garments could easily be mistaken for the late authoress. I suggest that one of you ladies puts them on, takes the next London train—making *quite* sure that you are noticed by a convenient porter—then, once under way, quickly resume your own garments, alight at the next halting point, discreetly dispose of the unwanted suiting, and return to Monument House. (*He looks around*) Do we all agree?

Emily Except for one thing.

Everyone looks at her

Little Goody Two-Shoes, upstairs. How do you intend to keep *her* quiet?

They all look at one another

She knows the Ash woman never left here alive. She's probably still trying to bring her round.
Lucien (*stunned*) She's right.
Dora She could ruin everything.
Monica (*coldly*) She could—but she *won't.*
Lucien You mean . . .?
Emily We're going to have to silence her. (*She flexes her fingers*)
Penworthy (*alarmed*) My dear Miss Emily. I'm sure we needn't advocate such drastic measures at *this* time. After all, Nurse Franklin stands to gain a not inconsiderable sum in return for her silence.
Emily Better to be sure than sorry. (*To Monica*) Fetch her.

Monica begins to move to the door. There is a sudden loud hammering from the outer door. Everyone jumps with shock

Dora (*her hand at her throat*) The police.

Penworthy shushes her with a motion of his hand, then passing Monica, moves to the doors and opens them a fraction to peer out. The hammering comes again

Penworthy (*looking back into the room*) Agatha. (*He puts one finger to his lips for silence, then turns back to the door*)

The sound of the outer door opening is heard

Perry (*off*) Hello. Sorry to bother you again—but I've had a bit of an accident.

Everyone reacts with shock

May I come in?

Penworthy flings the doors open wide and calls

Penworthy Who is it, Mrs Hammond? (*In mock surprise*) Good gracious. Mr Potter. (*He moves out into the hall*) My dear *boy*. Whatever has befallen you? Come in by the fire and dry yourself. Mrs Hammond, some towels if you please.

We hear the door close and Perry is escorted into the room by Penworthy. He has lost his coat, his trousers are wet and mudstained, duckweed and muddy water have soaked his shirt, his hair is plastered down and he has lost a shoe

Perry (*sheepishly*) I missed the turning at the end of the drive and went nose first into the river. Couldn't see a thing for the fog.
Monica (*coming to life*) You poor *darling*. You must be frozen. We must get you out of those wet things at *once*.

Before Perry can move, Monica has pounced on him and is unfastening his shirt

Perry (*startled*) Eh? (*He tries to break free*)
Monica (*struggling with the shirt*) You're so *cold*.

Penworthy Miss Monica.

Monica looks round at him

I am sure Mr Potter is perfectly capable of undressing *himself.*

Monica throws Penworthy a dirty look, then releases Perry, who backs quickly away from her

If you are indeed so anxious to help, then I suggest you try to find some suitable dry clothing for him.

Eyeing Perry like a starving dog would regard a fillet steak, Monica moves to the door

Monica I'll be right back.

Monica exits

Penworthy Now if Miss Emily would put another log on the fire . . .?

Emily moves up and puts another log on the fire

Thank you. (*To Perry*) We'll soon have the place warmed up again, Mr Potter. What a terrible experience for you.

Perry (*Shivering*) I'll say. Lucky I'm a good swimmer or I'd have been a gonner.

Penworthy (*catching Dora's eye*) Most fortunate. (*He leads Perry to the fireplace*) And so your vehicle is now at the bottom of the river?

Perry Sunk without trace. And if the doorcatch hadn't been faulty, I could have been down there with it.

Penworthy (*catching Emily's eye*) How—interesting.

Perry (*shivering*) Freda will be furious. She's only had it for just over a week. (*He looks round*) Where is she, by the way?

Lucien Freda?

Perry (*remembering*) Oh—er—I mean—Miss Ash.

Emily (*moving down to him*) I thought her name was *Ermyntrude*?

Perry (*edging away slightly*) Well—er—yes. It is. I mean—it's not—not exactly. It sort of *is* and it *isn't*, if you know what I mean.

Dora (*moving to him*) No, we don't. Perhaps you'd better tell us.

Penworthy (*with quiet menace*) Indeed you had.

Perry looks round dismayed at them as they hem him in

Perry (*uncomfortably*) Well—er—it's rather difficult. (*He looks about for a friendly face*) Perhaps she'd better tell you herself.

Lucien We'd much prefer to hear it from *you.*

Penworthy You see—Miss Ash is unable to tell us *anything* at the present time.

Perry (*gulping*) Well . . . (*He looks at them all in anguish*) It's quite simple really . . .

Emily It was "rather difficult" a few moments ago.

Perry (*trying to laugh*) Yes. Yes, it was, wasn't it? No—you see—the whole thing is—to be quite honest about it . . .

Dora And I do hope you *are* going to be honest, Mr Potter.
Perry (*gulping*) Yes. Of course I am. You see—her name isn't Ermyntrude Ash at all. It's Freda Mountjoy.

They all look at one another in grim satisfaction

Lucien Then what's happened to the *real* Ermyntrude Ash?
Perry (*backing into Emily*) Nothing. (*He recoils from her*) Nothing at all. That's just the name she *writes* under. Her pen name.
Penworthy (*light dawning*) Her *nom de plume*. (*He gives a relieved laugh and moves away from Perry*) Why—you had us all *worried* for the moment, Mr Potter.
Perry (*shakily*) I had me worried too.
Penworthy I'm afraid we assumed we were harbouring an impostor in our midst.

The others move sourly away

Perry (*his voice rising half an octave*) Impostor! (*He clears his throat*)
Penworthy Now I suggest you rid yourself of that wet clothing, and Mrs Hammond will see that it is dried, pressed and returned to you with all speed.
Perry (*looking at Dora and Emily*) Er . . .
Penworthy Ah, yes. The ladies. (*To them*) Perhaps you would care to leave the room for a few moments to allow our guest to disrobe? And if you could hurry Mrs Hammond along . . .

Agatha enters with a large wool blanket and a bath-towel

Ah, the good lady herself.
Agatha (*dourly*) Best I could manage. (*She thrusts them at Perry and stands*)
Lucien Thank you, Agatha. That will be all.
Agatha I'm waiting for his clothes.
Penworthy Mr Potter's clothing will be brought out to you in due course. Now if you wouldn't mind closing the doors behind you . . .

Agatha scowls, then turns on her heels and exits. Emily and Dora follow her, closing the doors

The room is all yours, Mr Potter.

Perry begins to peel off his shirt

Perry I never thought I'd be coming back here so soon. When I went over the edge, I thought my last hour had come. Thank goodness for the good old British workman. (*He drops the shirt*)
Lucien We expected you to be miles away by now.
Perry (*unzipping his trousers*) You—er—you didn't *mind* my coming back here, did you?
Penworthy But of course not. In fact, we're highly delighted that you *did* so. Had you not done, it could have created a rather delicate problem for us.

Perry (*puzzled*) Really? (*He takes off his trousers*)

Penworthy Without question. (*He takes the trousers*) See that Mrs Hammond has these at once, will you? (*He hands the trousers and shirt to Lucien*)

Perry It's going to be a delicate problem for me, too. Explaining to Freda about the car. (*He picks up the blanket*) You wouldn't mind telling her I'm back, would you?

Penworthy I—er—I don't think we'd better disturb her at the moment. The poor lady was—dead to the world when last I saw her.

Perry Lying down?

Penworthy Most certainly.

Lucien moves towards the door with the clothes. Anne comes hurrying in

Perry rapidly covers himself with the blanket

Anne (*flushed*) Mr Penworthy—I've got to talk to you. (*She sees Perry*) Mr Potter! I thought you'd gone.

Perry I fell in the river.

Lucien sniffs and exits

Penworthy If you would just excuse us a moment, Nurse? Mr Potter is changing.

Anne But I've got to speak to you. Now. It's important. That woman didn't die of a heart attack. She's been——

Penworthy (*quickly cutting in*) Nurse, Nurse. Please. To what lady are you referring? (*To Perry*) Excuse me. (*Drawing Anne out of earshot*) He doesn't know yet. I haven't been able to tell him.

Anne (*lowering her voice*) But she's been *poisoned.*

Perry looks startled, as he has *heard*

Penworthy Poisoned? Oh, come, come, Nurse Franklin. Aren't we being a little melodramatic? You can't be *certain* about that.

Anne (*her voice rising again*) She was drugged with some form of paralysing agent that caused her heart to stop. The symptoms are unmistakable. She's been *murdered*, I tell you.

Penworthy (*trying to quieten her*) But this is unbelievable.

Perry edges towards them slightly, to hear better

Anne (*firmly*) There's only one person could have been responsible for this, and we both know who it is, don't we?

Penworthy You cannot . . .

Anne (*more loudly*) It's Dora. (*Closing her eyes as if in pain*) I never really believed Emily's wild accusations about the home-made wines and the flower beds—but it's *true*, isn't it? Every word of it. Dora *kills* people.

Perry jumps

Penworthy (*gravely*) May I ask what you intend to do about it, Nurse?

Anne (*surprised*) I'm calling the police, of course. What else do you expect me to do? (*She turns and heads for the door*)

Penworthy Wait. (*He holds out his hand to detain her*)

Anne (*glancing round at him*) I think we've wasted enough time already.

Anne exits

Perry (*coming behind him*) Something wrong, is there?
Penworthy (*startled*) What? (*He turns*) Oh—Mr Potter. I'd forgotten about you I'm afraid. No. No, there's nothing wrong. Just a slight *technical* problem. Pray excuse me. I won't be a moment.

Penworthy turns and hurries out of the room

Perry looks after him, bewildered, then, closing the doors, returns to the fire and slips off his wet underwear, covered by the blanket

The panel swings open and Monica enters with a suit, shirt and other clothing

The panel closes as Monica moves behind Perry. He turns

Perry (*startled*) Ahhhhh!
Monica (*in a sexy voice*) I've brought you these. (*She moves closer*)
Perry (*nervously*) Oh—thank you. (*He looks for another door*) I—er—I didn't see you come in. (*He clutches the blanket tightly*)
Monica (*dropping the things on a chair*) That's because I came in the quick way. I didn't want you to catch—a chill.
Perry (*gulping*) That's—most thoughtful of you.
Monica (*moving in still closer*) Oh, I'm *very* considerate. (*She brushes his chest with her fingers*)
Perry (*backing away*) Really? (*He bumps into the table*)
Monica Would you like me to dry your back for you? (*She oozes closer*)
Perry (*his voice rising half an octave*) No thank you. I can manage.
Monica (*almost touching him with her body*) You've only to say the word.
Perry (*almost flat on the table*) Oh?
Monica And I'll do *anything*.
Perry I'm sure you would.
Monica (*straightening up*) Well now that you know I'm willing—(*She smoothes her gown*)—I'll just sit right here in case you change your mind. (*With a cat-like smile, she sinks on to a chair and gazes at him, licking her lips*)

Clutching the blanket tightly, Perry stands and reaches out for the trousers on the chair

Mmmmmmmmmmmm.
Perry (*startled*) Pardon?
Monica What a beautiful body you have.
Perry Oh—this old thing? (*He gives a nervous laugh*)
Monica (*rising*) Are you *sure* you don't need any help, Perry?
Perry (*retreating rapidly*) Positive, thank you.
Monica (*grabbing the blanket*) Peregrine. (*She tugs*)
Perry (*holding on*) No!
Monica (*heaving*) You're so sexy.
Perry (*frantically*) Get off! Let go!

The tussle is interrupted by the sound of three shots, off. Startled, Monica releases the blanket, stares at the doors, then hurrying to them, opens them

Monica (*calling*) What's happened? Who's shooting?

Monica exits

Dora (*off*) What is it? Who's shooting down there? Is it the police?

Perry quickly snatches up the trousers and scrambles into them under cover of the blanket

Emily (*off*) What's going on? Who fired?
Monica (*off*) Check the dining-room.
Dora (*off*) The police. It's the police. Help me, Lucien.

Anne appears in the doorway

Anne Mr Potter? Are you all right?
Perry (*spinning to face her*) Oh—yes. Yes. I'm fine. They—they came from out there.
Anne (*turning to look into the hall*) But who'd fire a gun in the *house*?

Emily enters

Emily Anything here?
Anne (*shaking her head*) It was out there.
Emily Upstairs.
Anne No. Dora's upstairs. She thought it came from down here.
Emily (*growling*) Dora doesn't know if she's on *this* earth or Fullers.

Lucien hurries into the room

Lucien This is monstrous. Monstrous! I will not have people shooting inside the house. Who was it? I demand to know.
Emily Oh, pipe down.

Dora comes scuttling in

Dora (*breathlessly*) Lucien, Lucien! What's happening? Why won't anyone tell me?
Emily Because we don't know, you old bird-brain. That's what we're trying to find out.
Anne (*suddenly*) Marcus. Where is he? Has anyone seen him?

Everyone looks blank

Alarmed, Anne hurries out

Anne (*calling*) Marcus! Marcus, where are you?
Marcus (*off*) Who is it in the press that calls on me?
Anne (*off*) Marcus. What on earth were you doing down there? You've not been bothering Oliver again, have you? (*She calls*) He was in the cellars.
Emily Best place for him. (*She moves away from the door*)
Marcus (*off*) Bid them prepare within. I am to blame to be thus waited for.

Anne and Marcus enter. Marcus is in his toga

Anne (*to Marcus*) We heard shots from somewhere and thought there'd been an accident. Then when we didn't see you . . .
Marcus (*patting her hand*) How foolish do your fears seem now, Calphurnia?

Perry stares at Marcus's toga

Perry Dress rehearsal, is it?
Marcus (*gazing at Perry with disdain*) He is a dreamer; let us leave him.
Lucien (*spluttering*) No-one's leaving this room until I find out who fired those shots. Who—and at what.
Emily Well unless someone makes a move, we're never going to find out. Where's Monica got to?
Dora (*gnawing her knuckles*) Perhaps Mr Penworthy . . .?
Lucien Yes. Where is the man? Has anyone seen him?
Anne He was in here with Mr Potter a few minutes ago.

They all stare at him

Perry (*gulping*) Maybe he went to—went to tell Freda I'd come back. She was lying down, he said. (*Worried*) I hope she's all right. She hates loud noises, and those shots were enough to waken the dead.
Emily That's wishful thinking, if ever I heard it.
Perry Pardon?

Anne looks at him a second, then comes to a decision

Anne Mr Potter. You've got to know sometime, so I think it's only fair to tell you that Miss Ash is . . .

She is interrupted by an ear-splitting scream from Monica, off

Lucien (*startled*) What?
Dora Monica . . .

As they all move to the door, the panel opens behind them and Penworthy steps into the room. He carries a gun on the end of a pencil. The panel closes behind him as he steps into the room

Emily It came from the cellars.
Penworthy One moment.

Everyone turns in surprise

There is no necessity for speed, I regret to say. Master Oliver is beyond human aid.
Anne Oliver?

The others react

Penworthy Shot down by an unknown assailant, whilst chained in his cell. (*He indicates the gun*) I found this in the passage.
Dora (*stunned*) Oliver. Oh, no.

Wordlessly, Lucien staggers to the drinks table and pours himself a drink

Emily (*holding out her hand to Penworthy*) Let me see that.

Penworthy (*removing the gun from her reach*) There is no need for further inspection, Miss Emily. I have already identified the weapon as the property of your late father. The question is—who fired it? (*He looks at them all*)

Marcus (*sagely*) There's the point.

Perry (*hesitantly*) Excuse me—but—well—shouldn't you have left it where it was? I mean—won't the police mind?

Anne He's right. You shouldn't have touched it. You of all people should know better than that.

Penworthy Indeed I *do*, but the alternative was to leave it where it lay, thus affording the murderer a chance to return and retrieve it.

Emily Why should he want to do that?

Penworthy I suspect I inadvertently disturbed him in the course of his crime, thus causing him to drop the weapon. This being the case, we may have reason for rejoicing. If the murderer did not wear gloves, his fingerprints will still be on the gun—and we shall have him.

Lucien's glass falls to the floor. Five pairs of eyes focus on him

Agatha enters the room, her lips pursed

Agatha Who did it? Who killed him? (*Spotting the gun*) That gun—it belongs to the Master. You've no right to touch it. Give it here. (*She holds out her hand*)

Penworthy I found it by Oliver's cell, Mrs Hammond. We suspect it has the murderer's fingerprints on it.

Agatha Then don't be such a fool, and wipe them off. You'll get no thanks for interfering in things that don't concern you.

Perry Wipe them off?

Anne You must be mad.

Agatha looks at her coldly

Agatha There's nothing wrong with *my* mind, Nurse Franklin, only one person in this household ever used that gun, and that's the Master.

Dora (*anguished*) But he's dead, Agatha. You know he is.

Agatha (*looking at her coldly*) Do I? What happened in that cellar tonight happened for the best in my opinion, and now I know it was the Master's doing I'm more than satisfied. So should you be. Now, take my advice, hand over that gun, dispose of the body, and forget all about it.

Penworthy (*indignantly*) I'm afraid your suggestion is quite out of the question, Mrs Hammond. Whatever your beliefs, a serious crime has been committed here and the wheels of the Law must be set in motion.

Perry Hear, hear.

Agatha (*like ice*) Very well. On your heads be it. But if this isn't what the Master wants, then there'll be even *more* deaths before this night is over.

(*She turns to the door*) I suggest one of you goes down there and helps Miss Monica with the body. We'll have dinner in ten minutes.

Agatha exits

Perry (*blankly*) Dinner?
Anne (*to Penworthy*) It'd better be me. I hope you realize how right I was, now?
Emily About what?
Penworthy I have been forced to accept Nurse Franklin's word that we have a double murderer hidden somewhere in the house.
Lucien Double?
Anne Oliver and Miss Ash, of course . . . (*She breaks off*) Oh.
Perry (*unable to believe his ears*) Freda? (*He looks at them all*) You mean—*my* Freda?
Anne (*contritely*) I'm sorry. I didn't mean to break it to you like that. I just didn't think.
Perry (*stunned*) Dead? But—she can't be. Not Freda.
Anne (*moving to him*) I'm sorry. Truly, I am.
Perry (*subsiding on to a chair*) But it's only a few minutes since I . . . (*Looking at Penworthy*) You told me she was lying down.
Emily We could hardly prop her up in a corner.

Anne throws a fierce look at Emily

Penworthy (*soothingly*) That, I'm afraid, was a foolish attempt on my part to conceal the fact of her demise from you——
Perry (*interrupting*) But why? (*He stands*) What *happened* to her?
Anne I think . . .

Penworthy holds up his hand to silence her

Penworthy As I am the instigator of this situation, I feel it is I who should do the explaining. If you will assist Miss Monica, Nurse Franklin, I will endeavour to tell Mr Potter the full story.
Anne (*nodding*) All right. But before I do anything, I'm going to have another try at getting through to the police. The sooner we get them out here, the better.

Throwing a sympathetic glance at Perry, Anne exits

Penworthy (*clapping Perry's shoulder*) If you would care to seat yourself once more . . .?
Perry (*shaking himself free*) Never mind about that. What happened to Freda?
Penworthy (*taking a deep breath*) She was—poisoned.

Everyone reacts

Lucien (*spluttering*) But you said she'd had a heart attack.
Emily (*glancing at Dora thoughtfully*) Poisoned!
Dora (*backing*) It wasn't me. It wasn't. They were all locked away. You know they were.
Perry (*to Penworthy*) How did it happen?
Penworthy Perhaps you'd better put on the rest of your clothes, Mr Potter.
Perry (*ignoring this*) Who poisoned *Freda*?

Penworthy I have no idea. At first we assumed that the shock of her inheritance had brought on a heart attack—

Perry Impossible!

Penworthy —but later, Nurse Franklin detected signs of poisoning, and informed me with all speed.

Perry Why didn't you tell me when I came back? Why all the secrecy?

Anne hurries back into the room

Anne The telephone. It's dead. I can't get a sound from it.

Penworthy (*turning to her*) Are you sure?

Anne Of course I am. There's not even a crackle.

Lucien Typical Post Office blundering. I shall put in a complaint at *once.*

Anne It was all right a few minutes ago. Before we heard the shots. I was getting the engaged signal. (*To Penworthy*) You—you don't suppose it's been—tampered with, do you?

Marcus What is't thou sayest?

Emily (*suspiciously*) You mean—the wires have been cut?

Anne I don't know. It's just dead.

Lucien (*peeved*) Vandalism. Sheer and utter vandalism. I shall go to the Prime Minister. To the very top. The *very* top.

Dora (*brightening*) Does that mean we can't call the police in now?

Anne (*firmly*) It means nothing of the sort. I'll get my coat on and walk down to the village. I can do it in half-an-hour.

Penworthy But the fog . . .

Anne Don't worry. I know the way blindfolded. (*She turns to leave*)

Perry (*suddenly*) I'd better come with you.

Anne (*turning back*) I'd rather you didn't, if you don't mind. I prefer everyone to stay right here. In the house. That way I know I'll be safe. (*She turns again*)

Penworthy (*stepping forward*) Just one moment, Nurse.

Anne looks round

Why should we let *you* walk out of here? For all we know, you could have poisoned Miss Ash and shot Master Oliver. (*Quickly*) Oh, I'm not *accusing* you—but how do we *know*? (*He beams*) Perhaps I had better go for the authorities.

Perry And how do we know that *you* didn't do it? You've got the gun.

Penworthy (*smiling thinly*) Mr Potter. Do I *look* like a murderer? (*He moves to the internal telephone and punches a number. After a moment he speaks*) Mrs. Hammond. My coat if you please. (*He hangs up*)

Emily Just a minute, Penworthy. Before you get carried away with your own importance. What proof have we that the Ash woman *was* poisoned? You've only *her* word for it. (*She indicates Anne*)

Lucien Emily's right.

Anne (*coldly*) I *do* happen to be a trained nurse, Miss Emily.

Dora She could have made a *mistake.*

Anne I'm not in the habit of making mistakes, Miss Dora. That woman was poisoned, and we're all aware of who did it.

Penworthy We *suspect*, Nurse Franklin.

Anne We *know*. She was poisoned by Miss Dora, deliberately and intentionally to prevent her from leaving this house.

Everyone reacts. Dora cringes

Penworthy (*annoyed*) You have no right to make such an accusation with out proof or reason.

Anne Reason? If that poor woman had left this house after accepting her legacy, *she'd still be alive*! Can you deny that?

Penworthy (*heatedly*) And who says that she *did* accept it, my dear Nurse? Were you listening at the keyhole, perhaps?

Anne (*scornfully*) There was no need. It's obvious she accepted. If she'd left here alive the rest of us would have been penniless. She had to be killed to prevent that happening.

Dora How dare you?

Perry (*stunned*) You mean . . .? (*He covers his face*) Oh, no. No. It couldn't have been. (*He sinks into the chair again*)

Emily And what about Oliver? Are you suggesting she killed him, too?

Anne Why not? That way there'd be one less to share the money with.

Penworthy (*firmly*) Nurse Franklin. You have accused Miss Dora of the most heinous of crimes, with nothing but suspicion to support you. The death of Miss Ash could possibly—I say possibly—have been the result of accidentally partaking of home-made wine, but—

Agatha enters with Penworthy's coat and scarf

—your assumption that the family needed her death to regain their fortune is quite incorrect. Nothing could be further from the truth. (*He begins to get into his coat*)

Lucien (*interested*) What was that, Penworthy?

Penworthy Being a layman, so to speak, Nurse Franklin would not know of a certain legal point which regrettably I have concealed from you all up to now. In a case like this—where the deceased person's assets prove insufficient after death duties, etc., to fulfil the terms of the Will, the amount that *does* remain is divided between the beneficiaries in as near the original proportions as intended.

Dora So the missing millions are ours after all? (*She beams*)

Penworthy A goodly portion of them, at least. The house alone would have passed to Miss Ash, plus what coinage remained after the division of the estate.

Lucien Then why didn't you tell us this before? Letting us think we were penniless? This is an outrage, Penworthy. An absolute outrage!

Anne What difference would it have made? Nothing he's said has changed a thing. That woman had still got to die. Dora couldn't take the risk of her discovering what she'd got buried in the garden.

Lucien (*fuming*) Nurse Franklin. I refuse to listen to any more of your vile accusations. You may leave this house at once. At once, do you hear?

Anne (*snapping*) With pleasure.

Penworthy One moment. Apart from myself, I regret that no-one must leave this house until my return with the police. Any attempt to do so will be viewed by them with great suspicion. Is that understood?

There is a moment's pause

Good. (*To Agatha*) Has the fog cleared at all, Mrs Hammond?

Agatha (*with gloomy relish*) Thicker than ever.

Penworthy Then the sooner I begin, the better.

Penworthy gives a slight bow, and exits, followed by Agatha. The doors close behind them

Lucien (*pulling the curtains back to look out*) Blasted stuff. It's all these *Government* experiments, if you ask me.

Emily (*growling*) I'll lay you ten-to-one he loses himself before he gets to the gates.

Anne (*to Marcus*) Come along, Marcus. I think we'd better put you back into your suit again. (*She takes his arm*)

Dora Why? What's wrong with him the way he is?

Anne (*coldly*) The police may want to question him when they arrive.

Lucien Why should they? He hasn't done anything. It's quite obvious to me, at any rate, that *this* pair of murders has absolutely *nothing* to do with the family. They were the work of a complete outsider.

Dora Hear, hear.

Lucien (*glaring at Perry*) And we all know there's only one outsider present, don't we? (*Loudly*) Him!

Perry (*looking up*) Eh?

Dora (*hissing at him*) Murderer!

Anne Oh, don't be such a fool, Dora.

Lucien She's not. We never had murders here before *he* arrived. Never.

Dora Ours were all accidents and suicides.

Emily And besides—none of the family would have *shot* Oliver. It's far too messy for us. It's *got* to be him.

Perry (*rising in horror*) But it wasn't. It wasn't! I wouldn't know how to begin to kill someone.

Dora (*smugly*) Just as I thought. A total lack of imagination.

Anne This is incredible. How you can stand here and accuse this poor man, I just don't know. In the first place, he wasn't even here when Miss Ash was poisoned, and as for killing Oliver—he wouldn't have known how to *find* him in that maze of corridors.

Emily Unless he had help—from another outsider. (*She looks pointedly at Anne*)

Anne (*taken aback*) You're surely not suggesting that I . . .?

Emily Why not? As you so beautifully pointed out when you accused Dora here—none of us—including yourself—thought we'd get anything unless the Ash woman died. Who better than a nurse to slip her a dose of something deadly? Hmmm?

Anne (*coldly*) An interesting theory, Emily, but you seem to have forgotten something. My job is to *save* lives—not take them.

Emily (*coolly*) So was Doctor Crippen's. (*She moves to the door*) I'll be in my room if the police want to see *me*.

Emily exits

Lucien I too see no reason for remaining in your company, Nurse Franklin. As soon as this criminal is arrested and removed from these premises, I shall be obliged if you will pack your bags and follow him. Come, Dora.

Lucien exits

Dora (*glaring at Perry*) Bluebeard!

Dora exits

Anne (*after a pause*) I—I'm sorry.
Perry (*dazed*) They're mad as hatters. All of them.
Anne (*throwing a quick glance at Marcus*) Mr Potter . . .
Perry How do you stand it? Being cooped up with them? Miles from anywhere? Aren't you afraid?
Marcus Of all the wonders that I have yet heard, it seems to me most strange that men should fear; seeing that death, a necessary end, will come when it will come.
Anne (*turning*) Marcus . . .
Marcus What can be avoided, whose end is purpos'd by the mighty gods?
Anne (*gently*) Go to your room and change, dear. I'll be up in a moment. I've got to talk to Mr Potter.
Marcus (*gravely*) Caesar shall forth.

Marcus bows deeply, and exits

Anne (*to Perry, gently*) Look. I know this has all been a terrible shock for you. It has for *all* of us, too. I'm sure we never expected anything like this to happen when you arrived, but I'd just like to tell you that . . . (*She breaks off*)
Perry (*puzzled*) Something wrong?
Anne (*gazing at the window*) There's someone in the garden. (*She goes to the window and tries to peer out*)
Perry Eh? (*He moves up to join her*)
Anne (*rubbing the glass*) I could have sworn I saw someone. Just there. By those shrubs. (*She peers*)
Perry (*doubtfully*) Are you sure?
Anne Well—I suppose it could have been a trick of the light, but . . . (*Eagerly*) Look. There it is again. It *is* someone (*She unfastens the window and opens it*) Who's there? Who is it?
Perry (*peering over her shoulder*) I can't see a thing. (*He shivers*) Brrrr.
Anne (*turning to him*) Wait here. I'm going to get a torch.
Perry You're not going out there alone, are you?
Anne Why not? I want to know what's going on. (*She moves past him*)
Perry I'll come with you. (*He turns and stoops to pick up the blanket*)

A shot rings out. Anne screams and staggers back. Perry spins round in fright

Are you all right? (*He runs to clasp her*)

Anne (*shocked*) He tried to kill me. He tried to kill me.

Perry (*looking over his shoulder*) Who did? Who was it?

Penworthy appears in the window opening. He carries the gun which is pointing at Perry

Anne (*trying to pull free of Perry*) No! No!

Perry's hands rise into the air as he turns to face Penworthy. Anne stands petrified. Penworthy steps into the room then slowly, crumples to the floor, a huge kitchen knife embedded in his back

Perry (*horrified*) Penworthy!

Perry's eyes glaze and he collapses in a dead faint. Anne begins to scream, as—

the CURTAIN *falls*

SCENE 2

The same. Early the following morning

The dining-room chairs have been removed and replaced with a chaise-longue. The body of Penworthy is gone. The window drapes have been opened to allow a weak daylight to filter through the thick shrubbery and the still dense fog

Lucien sits at the writing-desk slowly composing a letter. Emily, munching away at a large sandwich, is sitting perched on the edge of the library table watching him, whilst Monica is slumped in the wing-chair, a half-glass of brandy in her hand

Emily (*after a moment*) Who're you writing to, Lucifer?

Lucien (*looking up*) The Prime Minister, of course. And don't call me by that ridiculous name again. You know I don't like it. (*He goes back to his writing*)

Emily (*thoughtfully*) Prime Minister, eh? (*She takes a huge bite of her sandwich then turns to Monica*) I wonder how many crackpot letters *do* get sent to him each week?

Monica ignores her

A couple of hundred, would you say? More?

Monica remains silent

Hey, cloth-ears. I'm talking to you.

Monica (*snapping*) I can hear you.

Emily (*snarling*) Then why the hell don't you answer me?

Monica Because I'm thinking, that's why. (*She tosses her drink back in one gulp*)
Emily (*sneering*) Stinking's more like it. You've done nothing but guzzle that muck since you came down this morning.
Monica Go stick your feet in the trough. (*She pours herself another*)
Emily That's what I like about this family. We're all so friendly first thing in the morning.
Monica (*turning*) What's happened to the man? Peregrine?
Emily (*smirking*) Oh, so that's what's bothering you, is it? Little Pansy Potter. (*She heaves herself off the table*) Bit early in the day—even for you, isn't it?
Monica (*lurching to her feet*) You pig-faced old . . .
Emily (*easily*) He's having his poor little heady-weaddy patched up again. Down in the sick-room. Seems he bashed it about rather badly last night when he fainted. (*She chortles*) "My Hero." One whiff of blood and he's out like a light.
Lucien (*looking up*) How do you spell "outrage"? One "Y" or two?
Emily (*glancing at him*) One, you illiterate.

Monica puts down her glass and heads for the doors

And where are *you* off to, my pretty maid?
Monica Mind your own business.
Emily (*grabbing her arm as she passes*) It *is* my business. Everything that happens in this house is my business. Now where are you going?
Monica (*wrenching herself free*) Keep your greasy hands to yourself, Pig-face. If you must know, I'm going to have a few words with him. In private.
Emily (*grinning*) Oh, yeah? And what *else* did you have in mind?

Monica's hand comes up to slap her, but Emily grabs it

Careful, darling—or I might snap it off at the wrist.
Monica (*wrenching herself free again*) I want to talk to him about last night.
Emily What about it?
Monica (*defiantly*) I've found out something he ought to know.
Emily Like what, for instance?
Monica (*sullenly*) Like who's been behind all this. The murders and everything.

Lucien stops writing and turns

Emily (*dangerously quiet*) You mean—you *know*?
Lucien (*rising*) Who is it?
Emily Quiet, Lucien. I'll ask the questions.
Lucien (*his voice rising*) But I *demand* to know. As head of this household, I have every right to . . .
Emily (*savagely*) Be *quiet*!

Lucien's eyes pop with shock

(*To Monica*) Who is it?

Monica (*steadily*) You mean—you don't know, sister dear?
Emily (*pouncing on Monica's arm and wrenching it*) Who is it?

Monica screams with pain

Monica (*crying out*) Emily . . .

Emily twists harder and Monica screams again

Agatha enters, her face grim. She carries a meat-axe stained with blood

Agatha (*sharply*) Emily!

Emily glowers at her

Release Miss Monica's arm, if you please.

Emily remains as if frozen

I said *let go*!

Grudgingly Emily releases Monica, who reels back clutching her arm

That's better. Now, what was all that about?
Emily (*savagely*) Get knotted.

Agatha strides over to her in one movement and slaps her sharply across the cheek

Agatha (*calmly*) I'll remind you again, Miss Emily. We'll have no temperaments in this household. When I ask a question I expect an answer.
Lucien (*cowed*) Monica said she knew who'd done the murders, and Emily was trying to fi——
Agatha (*cutting him off*) I see. (*She looks at Monica*) And what were you intending to *do* with your knowledge?
Monica (*holding her arm*) I . . . (*Tiredly*) Oh, what's it matter?
Agatha Exactly. What we know, and what we think we know, are best kept to ourselves. We want no more deaths in this house unless they're *natural* ones. Is that understood?
Monica (*turning away*) Well you don't have to worry about that, do you? There *won't* be. It's all over.
Lucien Over? Over? How can it be, when that man's still in our midst? We could all be murdered in our beds. In my view, I hold him entirely responsible for what's happened here. I've told the Prime Minister so, too. In that letter—(*he points to the desk*)—I've demanded an immediate arrest.
Agatha I'm sure you have, Master Lucien. But there'll be no arrests. Everything is under control, so there's no need for outsiders to be brought into this. It will be our secret.
Emily (*glaring at her*) Fat chance of that. Not with Florence Nighty-light and that pansy secretary running around loose.
Agatha But they won't *be* running around loose, will they, Miss Emily?
Monica (*sharply*) What do you mean?

Agatha Have you all forgotten? *There's an empty car at the bottom of the river.*

Realization dawns on them all

Monica No. Not Perry!

Agatha (*calmly*) Oh yes, Miss Monica. Two "accidental" but perfectly "natural" deaths, and I think you will find that all the loose ends are quite nicely tied up. Think about it. (*With a change of tone*) Will you all be requiring morning coffee?

Before they can answer, Dora scuttles into the room, wearing her house-coat over a nightgown

Dora (*brightly*) Good morning, everyone. (*To the painting*) Father.

They all mutter greetings as she hurries over to the window to peer out

Oh, just look at it out there. So lovely and thick. (*She turns to them*) It's simply *perfect* for the funerals.

Lucien *What* funerals?

Dora Why—theirs, of course. I've thought of the most marvellous place for them. Under the rose bushes by the south wall. They've been looking so sickly these last few months. It'll put some body into them. (*She giggles at her own joke*)

Monica (*acidly*) I'm digging no graves today. Not in that lot.

Dora (*her lips quivering*) But—but we've got to bury them. We can't leave them lying around for the police to find.

Agatha Miss Dora's right. They can't stay in the house. Not if our plan is to go ahead.

Emily Oh, stick 'em in the vault for the time being. No-one ever goes creeping down there these days.

Lucien (*protesting*) But two of them are outsiders. And one's a perfect stranger.

Emily So what? I doubt if they'll try to steal anything.

Dora (*to Lucien*) Emily's right, dear. The vaults would be a *good* place for the time being. We can always have a proper funeral when the weather brightens.

Lucien (*annoyed*) The family vaults are for the exclusive use of this family. Let one outsider have the use of it, and the next thing we know, they'll *all* be clamouring to get inside. (*Fiercely*) It could even be nationalized!

Dora (*pleading*) It's only for a short while, dear.

Lucien (*peeved*) Oh, all right. Do what you wish. Don't mind *me*. I'm only the eldest. (*He returns to the desk and sits*)

Dora (*distressed*) Lucien . . .

Monica (*moving to the door*) We'd better get it over with before Nursey turns up. There's no point in waiting for *her* to give us a hand.

Agatha And besides—she may as well make the most of the few hours she's got left. (*Turning*) Coffee will be ready in ten minutes.

Agatha exits

Emily We'll take 'em through the tunnels. I don't fancy roaming round the gardens. Not with fog about.

Monica (*sneering*) Worrying about that precious skin of yours again, dearie? I've told you. We're all safe now. The killings are over.

Dora Oh? (*She looks from one to the other*)

Monica There won't be any more.

Dora opens her mouth as if to say something, then stops herself

Dora (*brightly*) I'll get the torches, shall I?

Lucien (*looking up and turning*) Torches? Torches? Why do you need torches? There's a perfectly adequate electric-light system in this house, isn't there?

Emily There will be if ever it gets finished.

Lucien (*rising*) What? But—but—this is intolerable. We paid——

Monica (*cutting in*) There hasn't been an electrician near the place since last summer. If you remember, Dora served them home-made sherry and seed cake during their tea-break—so they never quite managed to finish things. We've got them under the marigolds. Why do you think that damn generator's been clanking away for the last six months?

Lucien glares at Dora speechless, then fuming, sits heavily

Lucien (*muttering*) I won't have it. I won't *have* it.

Dora (*timidly*) I'm sorry, Lucien. I thought they'd finished.

Lucien (*still muttering*) I shall send in a complaint at once. (*Louder*) At once, do you hear. (*Very loudly*) At once. (*He grabs up his pen and begins to stab savagely at the paper*)

Emily (*to Monica*) Who're we going to take first?

Dora (*timidly*) Ladies first, wouldn't you say?

Monica (*heavily*) Come on.

Monica exits. Emily lumbers after her. Dora hesitates as if to speak to Lucien, but he ignores her so she slowly exits

Lucien scribbles on, with much grunting and emphasis

Lucien (*mumbling*) Incompetence—absolute fortunes—disgraceful . . .

The internal telephone rings. Lucien ignores it, concentrating on his letter. The telephone persists. With an angry snarl, he snatches it up

(*On the telephone*) Hello? . . . Who? . . . Yes, yes. . . . Of course it's me. Who did you think it was? . . . What? . . . My laboratory? . . . How dare they? How dare they. I shall come at once. Immediately.

Lucien slams down the telephone and scuttles out of the room

Marcus (*off*) Forget not, in your speed, Antonius, to touch Calphurnia; for our elders say, the barren, touched in this holy chase, shake off their sterile curse.

Lucien (*off*) Get out of my way, you—you LUNATIC!

Marcus enters the room. He is in his toga

Marcus (*grandly*) Nor heaven nor earth have been at peace tonight: Thrice hath Calphurnia in her sleep cried out, Help, ho. They murder Caesar. (*He looks about him*) Who's within?

Seeing no-one, he turns and closes the door. He then moves to the table and rifles through Penworthy's deeds box. Extracting a handful of the papers, he begins to read quickly, dropping the discarded ones on to the floor. As he stands with his back to the panel, it begins to open. A gloved hand holding the gun is pointed at his back. With a sudden grunt, Marcus finds what he is looking for and turns. The gun is fired. He staggers and with an effort looks into the opening

Et tu, Brute. (*He crumples to the floor*)

The gun is tossed into the room and the panel closes. For a moment there is silence

The doors burst open and Agatha hurries in. She sees Marcus

Agatha Mr Marcus! (*Hurrying to his side, she stoops over him*) Oh, no. Not you, too! (*Looking up at the portrait*) Why, Mr Septimus? Why *him*? (*Seeing the gun, she picks it up and stands holding it*)

Perry, a large dressing on his head, hurries in

Perry (*breathlessly*) What was it?

Agatha turns, gun pointed at Perry

Aaaaah! Don't shoot! (*His hands fly into the air*)

Agatha (*stunned*) He's dead.

Perry (*petrified*) It doesn't matter. I won't tell anyone. Promise.

Agatha Murdered, (*She looks down at Marcus. Her eyes sharpen. Stooping down again she prises the paper out of Marcus's hand and glances at it*)

Perry remains frozen by the door

So *that*'s it.

Anne comes scurrying in

Anne (*Breathlessly*) What's happened? Who fired . . . (*She sees Marcus and lets out a startled gasp*) Marcus! (*Pushing Agatha aside, she dashes to him and flings herself down beside him*) Marcus!

Perry She's shot him.

Anne presses her ear to Marcus's chest

Anne (*looking up*) He's still breathing. Quick! Get me some clean towels and a blanket. (*She begins to unfasten the toga*) And some dressings. (*She peels away the toga top*) Oh, God . . . (*To Agatha*) Hurry, woman. (*She bends over him again*)

Agatha looks at Anne blankly for a moment, then snaps out of it and hurries from the room, still holding the gun and the crumpled paper

Perry (*looking after Agatha*) You—you're not going to let her run round loose with that thing, are you?

Anne (*working on Marcus*) Don't be so stupid, Perry. She didn't shoot him. She worshipped the ground he walked on.
Perry (*protesting*) But the gun . . .?
Anne (*irritatedly*) She probably picked it up from the floor. (*With a sudden change*) Let me have your coat. I want a cushion for his head.

Perry reluctantly takes off his coat and gives it to her. She folds it and slips it under Marcus's head

Thank you.
Perry You—you won't get blood on it, will you? It's the one I borrowed.

Anne glares at him

Sorry. (*He peers at Marcus*) Is he going to be all right?
Anne (*testily*) How should I know. He's bleeding like fury, and the bullet's still inside him. (*Impatiently*) Where is she with those things?
Perry Shouldn't we try to get him upstairs, or something?
Anne Are you mad? He hasn't a dog's chance if we move him now. (*She goes back to working on Marcus*;
Perry (*thoughtfully*) I wonder what that paper was. The one that Agatha took off him?
Anne Paper?
Perry Yes. It looked like a certificate, or something. He had it in his hand. She seemed very interested in it.
Anne (*brushing it aside*) Couldn't have been anything important. The poor boy wouldn't know one . . .

Agatha enters with towels, a blanket, bowl of water and first-aid box

Quickly, Anne takes them from her and begins to pad out the wound and staunch the blood

Perry (*looking away*) I think I'm going to be sick.
Anne Then try to do it quietly. (*She carries on working*) Pass me the water.
Agatha (*handing her the bowl*) It's no use, I tell you. He's dead.
Anne (*tartly*) Leave the nursing to me, will you, and stick to running the household. Where are the others?
Agatha Taking the other bodies down to the vaults.
Anne (*turning round and looking at her with shock*) Doing *what*? Those bodies mustn't be touched until the police arrive.
Perry (*sitting weakly*) If they ever do.
Anne (*grimly*) They'll arrive all right. As soon as I've got this wound under control, I'm going down to the village for them myself.
Perry (*startled*) No! You can't. Remember what happened last night?
Anne I've got to, Perry. If he doesn't get expert medical attention soon, he's going to die. He hasn't a chance with that bullet inside him.
Agatha He hasn't a chance anyway. The poor lamb's dead.
Anne Will you stop *saying* that? If we only can get him to a hospital he'll be fine. I *know* he will.
Agatha (*in a more gentle tone*) It's no use trying to fool yourself, Miss. He's done for and you know it.

Anne If you say that once more, I'll—I'll slap you! Now get out of here, and get me my coat!

Perry Wait, Anne. Let me go for the police. You'd better stay here and look after him. I mean—you can't leave him on his own can you? (*He rises*)

Anne I don't intend to. *You* can watch him for me. You seem to be the only one I can trust.

Perry But what if the killer comes after *you*? To stop you.

Anne (*after a slight pause*) I'll take the gun. He wouldn't dare try anything then.

Agatha (*drawing herself up*) There'll be no need for that. *I*'ll go. I see now I've been wrong. It's obvious he needs help, and he'll not harm me, no matter what he's done to the others.

Perry (*puzzled*) Who won't?

Agatha The Master, of course. He's a sick man.

Anne For the last time, Agatha . . .

There is a loud wailing from Dora. A moment later, she comes scuttling through the doors in great distress

Dora He's gone. Gone! (*She grabs at Agatha's arm*) The coffin's open and he's gone. (*She sees Marcus and gives a cry*) Marcus . . .!

Anne (*sharply*) He's been wounded, that's all. He's going to be fine. (*She rises*) Now calm down and speak clearly. Who's gone? Whose coffin is open?

Dora (*wailing*) Father's.

Anne looks at her in astonishment. Dora pulls away and collapses on to the chaise

Without a word, Agatha executes an about-turn and exits

Perry (*groaning*) Oh, no. Not body-snatching as well.

Dora (*sniffing*) The lid was on the floor. Absolutely shattered. It was horrible. Horrible. (*She breaks down*)

Perry (*trying to comfort her*) There, there.

Dora (*weeping*) People just don't realize how expensive good marble is, these days.

Perry gives her a startled look

Anne And you say the body is missing?

Dora (*nodding*) He's been stolen. I know he has. (*She sobs again*)

Anne (*tightly*) That's if he were ever in there to start with. From the beginning, Agatha's been convinced the funeral was a put-up job, and the Old Man didn't *really* die. Now it's beginning to look as though she's right. Where did she go?

Perry Down the hall, I think. To the kitchen.

Anne (*stooping to cover Marcus with the blanket and check him*) Stay here with Dora and keep an eye on Marcus. He'll be all right for a little while, but don't leave the room *under any circumstances*. Understand?

Dora (*looking up*) What are you going to do?
Anne I'm going to find your father.

Anne exits hurriedly

Dora (*beginning to weep again*) I don't understand what's going on. Why is everyone dying like *this*? It simply isn't amusing any more.
Perry (*startled*) Amusing?
Dora (*sadly*) It wasn't like this in the old days. We had finesse then.
Perry (*gulping*) Really?
Dora That's how we made the family millions. People *trusted* us. It was all done with charm and discretion. There was never a *suggestion* of suspicion from anyone.
Perry Oh?
Dora (*sniffing*) Of course, you wouldn't know, would you? But we're direct descendants of the Borgias. Oh, yes. Alexander's sister Marcella married Guiseppe de Tombra just four weeks before he died. It was her first success. No-one suspected a thing, and that in itself was rather remarkable, for those times. She was a lady who liked to travel, and eventually came to England with her son Marcus, anglicized her name and went into business. Naturally, in a backward place like this, she was a great success. The Italian methods were very popular. Even the Royal Family . . . (*She coughs and breaks off*) We've always tried to live up to her standards—even during the last few years—and now *this* has to happen. All these *common* murders. And all in one night. (*She weeps again*)

There is a loud frantic scream, off, from Anne. It is followed by a second one. Perry and Dora jump. Perry hurries to the door, remembers Marcus, turns, goes back, then turns to exit again

Anne comes staggering in, her uniform blood-spattered

Anne (*hysterically*) Perry! Perry! Take me away from here! Take me away! (*She throws herself into his arms in a state of collapse*)
Perry What is it? What's happened?
Anne (*sobbing violently*) She's dead. In the kitchen. He did it with the meat-axe. It was *horrible*. (*She sobs*)
Dora (*standing shakily*) Agatha?
Anne (*fighting to control herself*) She was behind the door. I couldn't see her at first, then she slid down. Right into my arms. (*She buries herself into Perry's shoulder*) Ohhhh!
Dora (*puzzled*) I don't understand. She said there'd be no more. She *promised*. We only had to dispose of you two.

Perry gives Dora a startled look, then leads Anne to the wing-chair

Perry Sit down. I'll get you a drink.

Anne collapses into the chair while Perry pours her a drink. He hands it to her

Here. It'll do you good.

Anne is about to take a sip, when suddenly she realizes, and thrusts it violently from her

Anne No. No, I don't want it.
Perry (*looking at the glass*) Eh?
Anne (*trembling*) It could be poisoned.
Dora (*indignantly*) It's best Madeira.
Anne I don't care what it is. I'm not eating or drinking anything in this house. (*She forces herself to her feet*) We've got to get away from here. Now.
Perry But what about him? (*He indicates Marcus*)

Anne looks at Marcus, clenches her knuckles to her mouth, looks at Perry in horror

Anne We can't. We *can't* leave, can we? Not with him like that. We're trapped.
Perry We could always leave him till we got help.
Anne *No*. He's not staying alone in this house. I—I've got an idea now of what's going on. (*More steadily*) It's quite obvious that the late Mr Tomb isn't late at all. He's very much alive and completely insane.
Dora (*outraged*) How dare you?
Anne (*ignoring her*) For reasons best known to himself, he's only been *pretending* to be dead—thus giving him the chance to murder his family and employees in absolute safety.
Perry But that's ridiculous, Anne. He couldn't have fooled the doctor *and* the undertaker. Not to mention old Penworthy.
Anne (*triumphantly*) And who says he did? (*Eagerly*) Don't you see, Perry? He *bribed* them to keep quiet. Then they'd say anything he told them to. It's the answer to everything.
Perry But what about Freda? Where does she fit in?
Anne (*her mood collapsing*) I don't know. (*Thoughtfully*) You're quite sure they'd never met before?
Perry Positive. She'd never even set eyes on him.
Anne (*frowning*) But there must have been *some* connection. That story about the books was too ridiculous for words.
Perry (*insistently*) But there wasn't.
Anne There *has* to be. Or why include her in the Will?
Perry Why include her in the Will if he's going to kill her? It doesn't make sense. And anyway . . .
Anne (*eagerly*) I've got it. It was the only way he could get her to come to Monument House. By making her think he was dead.
Perry But I keep telling you. She'd never met him. Ever.
Anne Then . . . (*She breaks off*) Oh, I don't know. *You* think of something.
Perry All right. How about this? Tontine.

Dora and Anne look at him blankly

It's the perfect solution. Last survivor takes all.

Anne In the first place, a tontine is illegal, and in the second, what's the point? It's all his to begin with.
Perry (*crestfallen*) I didn't think of that bit.
Dora (*curiously*) But what if he's right? What if it *is* a tontine?
Anne (*patiently*) It can't be. Not with your father still alive.
Dora But what if he isn't? If he really *is* dead?
Perry Then . . .
Dora (*her eyes sparkling*) It must be one of the family, mustn't it? (*With great glee*) How beautiful. I should have realized, shouldn't I? It's the work of a genius. That fine Italian hand. The hand of a Tomb.
Perry Yes. A Tomb with a view—to polishing off everybody named in that Will. We've got to get out of here, Anne.

Monica enters, followed by Emily

Dora (*spotting them first*) Did you find him?
Emily Not a sign. Whoever took him from that vault did a good job of it. Unless he walked.
Monica Don't talk rubbish. He didn't walk anywhere.
Anne (*to Emily, sharply*) You're bleeding. (*She stares at Emily's hand*)
Emily Huh? (*She looks down and tries to rub the blood off*)
Anne Let me see. (*She moves towards her*)
Emily (*drawing away*) It's nothing. I must have brushed against something.
Perry (*staring at her*) Agatha!
Monica What about her?
Dora *She's* been murdered, too. With an axe.
Monica (*stunned*) But—she *can*'t have been.
Dora (*eagerly*) But she has. And Marcus has been *shot*.
Monica It's impossible.

Anne looks silently at Marcus. Monica and Emily follow her glance and see him

Emily Dead?
Anne Not yet.
Monica (*hurrying to his side*) Marcus!
Anne (*sharply*) Don't touch him. He's lost a lot of blood.
Emily (*grabbing Anne's arm*) Who did it?
Anne (*pulling free*) That's what we'd all like to know.
Monica (*looking up*) He's dead. (*Her voice rising*) He's dead.

Anne hurries to her side and pushes her away. Kneeling beside Marcus, she puts her ear to his chest again to listen

Anne No. He's still holding on. But only just.
Monica He's as cold as a marble slab.
Anne I told you. He's lost a lot of blood. But you're right. He can't last much longer without help. We've got to do something.

Anne strokes Marcus's forehead, then puts another log on the fire. Pulling the blanket closer around him, she stands

Emily How did it happen?

Anne I don't know. Agatha found him, took the gun and went out. She must have run smack into the killer. He was waiting for her in the kitchen.

Monica But what was Marcus *doing* in here? And why are all these papers on the floor?

Emily (*her eyes darting*) The Will. He must have been after the Will. (*She begins to scrabble round, looking for it*)

Monica Never mind about that for the minute. What I want to know is, who killed Agatha and shot Marcus?

Anne Presumably the same person who killed the others. Your father.

Monica Rot. Father didn't kill him—or them. Penworthy murdered the first two—and *I* killed him.

Anne's eyes open wide. The others all look at Monica in fascination. Perry edges quickly away

I was watching him when he left the house. But instead of heading down the drive, he slipped into the shrubbery and began to make his way back here with the gun in his hand. I figured he was up to something, so I helped myself to one of the kitchen knives and slipped out after him. I arrived just in time to see him take aim, and got him before he had a chance to squeeze the trigger.

Dora (*breathing hard*) Oh, Monica.

Anne (*backing slightly*) So it was *you*! It was you all the time.

Perry You saved her life, Monica. He couldn't possibly have missed her from that distance.

Monica (*looking at him oddly*) He'd have missed her by a mile. He was aiming at you.

Perry looks startled

Anne (*suspiciously*) How do we know you're telling the truth? How can we be certain it didn't happen the other way round? That Penworthy spotted *you* in the garden, and you had to kill him to keep *him* quiet?

Perry (*surprised*) Anne!

Anne (*to Perry*) She could have moved her father's body from the vault and hidden it somewhere in the tunnels. Nobody knows their way round them like she does.

Monica (*scornfully*) You're out of your mind.

Anne Somebody is. One of you is a killer. A killer not content with murdering your own family, but slaughtering innocent outsiders as well.

Emily (*moving towards her*) Now just you listen to me . . .

Anne (*stepping back with a cry*) Don't touch me! Don't *touch* me. Well, I'm not going to be victim number six. You can have my share of the money, if that's what you're after. I don't want it. Not a penny. Do you understand? I just want to stay alive and get help for poor Marcus. Did you hear me? For Marcus. (*More controlled*) Now I'm going up to my room to get my coat, and then I'll be leaving for the village. Please don't follow me. Any of you. I shall be quite safe.

Monica How do you *know*?
Anne (*steadily*) Because I'll be taking the gun with me, and I'll shoot the first one of you I see coming after me.

Anne turns and almost runs out of the room

Perry (*coming to life*) Anne! Wait. Listen.

Perry hurries out after Anne

Dora Well, really.
Monica (*bitterly*) Aren't our nurses wonderful?
Emily (*easing her bulk on to the table edge*) I don't suppose there's any chance she was right, is there? About you doing a Pickfords job on Papa?
Monica (*snarling*) What do you think?
Emily I wouldn't put it past you, sweetheart. Not when there's a possibility of you getting your mitts on four million pounds.
Monica Listen to the pot. If anybody moved him out of that vault, you're the most likely suspect. You've got muscles like an ox.
Emily You don't need muscles if you've got a slate loose, dearie. Even Madam Defarge there—(*she indicates Dora*)—could manage that.

Dora bridles

(*To Dora*) I bet you could swing a nifty meat-axe in those birdlike talons, couldn't you?
Monica (*sweetly*) If she could, I'm sure *you'd* have found out about it *years* ago.
Emily And what about precious little Lucy-boy? Do you think *he*'s incapable of humping a corpse on his back? (*She frowns*) Where is he, by the way?
Monica What's it matter?
Emily I think it's time we all got our heads together and did some serious thinking. (*She moves to the door*) I'll go get him.
Monica Not by yourself, *sweet one*. We'll *both* go. Just to be safe.
Emily (*smirking*) And what makes you think you'll be safe with me?
Monica Because Dora will know we left here together. That's why.
Dora I'll come, too, if you like.
Emily We're not going on safari. You stay here and look after *him*. And if you hear anything—just scream.

Emily nods at Monica and exits. Monica follows her

Dora looks after them for a moment, hovering between following and obeying instructions. Then finally she closes the doors and moves up to Marcus

Dora Poor Marcus. So still and white. (*She touches him*) And cold. (*She looks anxious*) Warmth. He must have warmth. (*She puts a log on the fire*) Burn, burn, burn.

The door opens and Perry enters, looking glum

Perry She's locked herself in. Won't even listen to me. I heard her bolt the door.

Dora (*frowning*) Did you? Oh. How very unfortunate.

Perry Why's that?

Dora What if somebody decides to *kill her*?

Perry (*slumping into the chair*) He hasn't a hope. Those doors must be a foot thick. And soundproof.

Dora Ah, yes. But then—he wouldn't go in through the door, would he? He'd use the passage behind the fireplace. We hardly ever use the doors here, you know. The tunnels are much quicker.

Perry (*rising*) You mean—he can still get at her?

Dora (*smiling*) And we wouldn't even hear her scream.

Perry (*horrified*) Anne! Anne!

Perry dashes out of the room, calling madly

Dora (*looking after him*) Fool.

Dora suddenly gives a laugh. It is quite evil and unlike the image she has previously presented. With almost balletic grace, she moves to the doors and closes them again. As she does so, the panel behind her begins to open. With a little smile on her face, she turns and sees the opening. She gasps and goes rigid

Who's there? Who is it?

There is no reply. The panel remains open and clear

Lucien? (*With great caution she approaches the opening*) Hello? Is that you, Papa? (*She peers inside*) Hello?

Dora vanishes inside. For a moment there is silence, then the library doors open and Anne appears followed by Perry. She wears her outdoor coat

Anne (*as she enters*) Oh, don't be so ridiculous, Perry. I've told you I'll be all right and . . . (*She sees the room is empty and the panel is open*) Marcus! (*She rushes to his side*) Marcus?

Perry (*looking round, baffled*) But she was here a minute ago.

Anne (*looking up brokenly*) He's dead.

Perry (*moving to the panel*) Dora? Miss Tomb? (*To Anne*) She must have gone through here.

Anne (*springing up*) Dora? (*She hurries to the opening*) Dora, where are you?

As she vanishes into the opening

(*Off*) Dora? *Dora?*

Perry (*nervously*) Anne. Come back.

Anne reappears in the opening

Anne (*urgently*) Get some help. (*She hurries to the door and calls*) Everybody. Help! *Help!*

Perry (*anxiously following her*) Did you find her? Is she all right?
Anne There's not a trace. We've got to find her, Perry. She could be in danger. Terrible danger. (*She calls again*) Help!
Perry What are we going to do?
Anne We've got to go after her. Through the tunnels. There's not a minute to spare.

Monica enters breathlessly

Monica What's wrong? What's happened?
Anne It's Dora. She's gone. Into the passageways. And Marcus is dead.
Monica (*hurrying to the panel*) Dora? (*To Anne and Perry*) Come on. Follow me.

Emily blunders breathlessly into the room

Emily (*gasping*) What is it?
Monica (*snapping*) Dora. She's missing.

Dora suddenly appears in the opening. She is struggling with a fairly large cardboard box

Anne (*spotting her*) Dora!
Monica (*turning*) Where the *hell* have you been? We thought you were missing.
Dora (*contrite but excited*) I'm sorry. But the panel opened and no-one came out, so I went in.
Anne (*angrily*) You fool, Dora. You could have been killed. (*She looks at the box*) And what's that?
Dora I found it in the passageway. It's quite heavy.
Perry (*curiously*) What is it?
Dora I don't know. (*She totters to the table with it*) But it's got Father's writing on it. (*She puts it down*)
Emily (*her eyes sparkling*) His writing?
Monica But where did it come from? It wasn't there last night.
Dora (*eagerly undoing the wrappings*) Maybe it's the money?
Anne In that?
Perry (*grinning nervously*) Perhaps it's a *small* fortune?

Dora pulls out masses of tissue paper

Dora It's very carefully packed.
Emily Let me see. (*She tugs out more paper*)
Monica (*joining in*) Here. (*She pulls out even more tissue*)
Dora (*plaintively*) I found it. I found it.
Emily (*yanking out the last piece of covering*) Now let's have a look at what we've got . . . (*She peers inside and reacts violently. Releasing the box, she staggers back*)
Monica (*startled*) What is it? (*She peers inside and quickly turns away*), Ugh!

Dora gazes down into the box without emotion

Anne (*bewilderedly*) What is it? What's inside?
Dora (*in an odd sort of voice*) It's Lucien's head.

Dora begins to lift the head out of the box, as—

the CURTAIN *falls*

ACT III

The same. That evening

The room is as before, but the body of Marcus has been removed, as has also the box containing Lucien's head. The scattered papers have been gathered together and replaced in the deeds box. Blankets, towels and bowl of water are also gone. It is dark. The main lights are on and the fire is almost out. The main drapes are still open and the fog can still be seen.

Anne, in her uniform, is staring blindly out of the window, fingers drumming nervously on the panes. Dora in a fresh chiffon gown with long trailing scarf, is sitting in the wing-chair. Emily, a dish of apples by her side, is perched on the table edge, munching happily away at the remanant of an apple

Dora (*singing quietly*)
Four green bottles, hanging on the wall.
Four green bottles, hanging on the wall.
And if one green bottle, should accidently fall—
(*Getting louder*) There'll be three green bottles, hanging . . .

Anne (*savagely*) Dora! (*She turns and glares at her*)

Dora jumps, bridles, then sinks into silence

Emily (*with her mouth full*) Something wrong, Nurse?

Anne (*looking at her incredulously*) Wrong?

Anne closes her eyes and shakes her head tiredly before returning to gaze out of the window. There is a momentary silence which is broken by Emily sucking on the apple core. Anne turns away from the window

(*With loathing*) Why doesn't it *clear*? Why doesn't it *go*?

Emily (*glancing at her*) Feeling the strain, are we? Bit nervy?

Anne (*urgently*) We've got to get *help*, Emily. Before it's too late.

Emily (*sucking at the apple core*) For what?

Anne (*amazed*) Before there's another murder, of course.

Emily (*with an amused smile*) Oh? And who says there's going to be another? You? (*She drops the core on to the carpet*)

Anne looks down at it in disgust

Anne Well he's not going to stop now, is he? Not after going this far. Can't you see that? He's going to kill *all* of us. (*She turns away*) We've just got to get through to the police.

Emily (*selecting another apple*) So what's stopping you? (*She rubs the apple on her sleeve to polish it*)

Anne (*facing her again*) You *know* what's stopping me.

Emily Do I? (*She makes a great show of remembering*) Oh, yes. The gun.

It's vanished again, hasn't it? Pity about that. (*She takes a bite of apple*)

Anne (*amazed*) Is that all you can say? Can't you get it into your thick skull that we're all in deadly danger so long as that gun's unaccounted for? There's still a bullet left in it.

Emily Is that so? (*She munches*)

Anne (*to Dora*) It was there. On the kitchen table. I saw it with my own eyes. I'd have picked it up if Agatha hadn't—hadn't—fallen on me. (*She shudders at the memory*)

Emily Pity you got distracted, then, isn't it? You could have been miles away by now. (*She takes another bite, and looks off into the hall*) What's keeping those two? I'm starving.

Dora (*rising*) Perhaps I'd better . . .

Anne (*sharply*) No. No-one goes anywhere alone. Remember? That's what we agreed on, and that's how it's going to be.

Dora (*coldly*) It may be what *you* agreed on, Nurse Franklin, but *I* will make my own agreements, thank you very much.

Anne (*to Emily*) Emily. Tell her.

Emily Why should I? If she wants to go out there, she can do. *I* shall.

Anne (*shaken*) Then you're mad. You're just asking to be killed.

Emily *Nobody*'s going to be killed. (*With great emphasis*) There'll be no more deaths. (*Sourly*) Unless I die of starvation waiting for those blasted sandwiches. (*She bellows off*) Monica!

Perry (*off*) Coming. Coming.

Emily (*grunting*) And not before time, either. (*She heaves herself off the table*) They've been out there long enough to bake the bread. (*She takes a bite of her apple*)

Perry scuttles into the room with a large plateful of "doorstop" sandwiches. His hair is mussed, lipstick is plastered all over his features, his shirt and tie are askew, and his shirtflap is hanging out, though some attempt has been made to cram it back in again. Monica, a smile on her lips, sidles in behind him

Perry (*panting*) Sorry I took so long. I kept getting—(*he glances at Monica*)—sidetracked.

Monica blows a kiss at him

Anne (*coldly*) So I noticed.

Monica (*sweetly*) Well, you did say we had to keep our eyes on one another, didn't you, dear?

Anne Perhaps I should have mentioned *hands* off as well.

Perry (*jumping in*) Sandwich? (*He holds out the plate*)

Anne (*turning away*) No thank you. I'm not hungry.

Dora Well, I certainly am. (*She helps herself to one*)

Emily lifts the plate out of Perry's hand, takes two, and carries the plate off to the table with her

Perry (*following Anne*) You've got to eat something, Anne. It's been twenty-four hours.

Anne I don't care if it's been twenty-four months. I'm not eating or drinking a thing in this house, and that's final.

Perry But they're quite safe. Honestly. I made them with my own fair hands. Monica watched me.

Anne I'll *bet* she did.

Monica (*amused*) My, my. Look at those green eyes flashing. (*She moves over to the fire*)

Perry Oh, come on, Anne. You don't want to starve to death, do you? (*He realizes what he has said*) Sorry. (*As the thought strikes him*) Here . . . (*He turns and grabs the dish of apples*) Have one of these. Nobody can tamper with an apple (*He holds one out to her*)

Emily (*tossing down her sandwich and hurtling towards Perry*) Tell that to Snow White. (*She snatches the bowl and the apple from him*) These happen to be my property. If she wants apples she can get her own. (*She puts the bowl down on the table*)

Perry (*protesting*) You can spare *one*.

Emily For *her*? (*She sneers and bites into the apple*)

Anne (*quietly*) It's all right, Perry. I couldn't. Let her keep them.

Emily I intend to. (*She munches and chokes*)

Monica (*amused*) Didn't somebody once say something about pigs and acorns?

Emily continues to choke. The apple drops from her hands and falls to the floor. She clutches at her throat wildly trying to scream

Anne (*startled*) Emily . . . (*She springs forward and pounds her on the back*)

Emily's arms flail madly

Dora (*almost in a whisper*) Emily.

Emily gives a convulsive shudder and goes limp

Anne (*struggling to support her*) Perry. Quick!

With Perry assisting her, they lower Emily to the floor. Dora stands, hand clenched to her mouth; Monica, unmoving, by the fire

Stick your fingers down her throat. Quickly! *Quickly*. Let *me* do it. (*She pushes him aside*) I know . . . (*She stops. Her face registers bewilderment then she puts her face close to Emily's and sniffs hard*) Almonds. (*She sniffs again then rises in horror and backs slowly away from the body*) *Cyanide!* She's been poisoned with cyanide!

Everyone looks at her

It was in the apple. (*To Perry*) The one you were trying to give to *me*. (*She looks at him in horror*)

Perry (*stunned*) Anne.

Anne (*retreating towards the doors*) You were trying to kill me. And if it hadn't have been for her (*She glances at Emily*) you *would* have done.

Perry (*aghast*) No! (*He moves towards her*) Anne. Listen to me.
Anne (*terrified*) Keep away from me!

Anne turns and dashes out of the room

Perry (*half pursuing her*) Anne! Come back!
Dora (*to Perry*) Murderer!
Perry (*turning*, *startled*) Eh?
Monica (*amused*) Don't panic, lover boy. I know you didn't pull *this* one. Not unless you're a damn sight cleverer than you look.
Perry Oh, I'm not. Honestly, I'm not.
Monica I've seen the way you look at the pretty Miss Franklin. Like a moonstruck cow. Wish I knew how she did it. (*She shakes her head*) No—you'd not take the chance of *her* sinking her dainty little teeth into a poisoned apple.
Dora (*tartly*) Well, *someone* must have done it.
Monica (*smiling secretly*) Yes. And there aren't many of us left, are there? Still—it's one less to share the spoils with when we find them.
Dora Monica . . .
Monica (*glancing at her*) There's nothing of the hypocrite about me. I hated her guts and she hated mine. (*Wryly*) Besides—maybe the side effect will benefit us all. It's probably saved the country from a famine.
Dora (*shocked*) She was your sister!
Monica And now she's my *late* sister.

Dora turns away in distress, moving to the window. She gives a startled gasp

Dora Look. (*She points outside*)

Perry and Monica move to the window

Perry The fog. It's lifting. We can leave. (*He turns*)
Monica Wait.

Perry turns again

Don't you think you ought to leave it a little longer? Just to make sure.
Perry Are you kidding? I'm going up to get Anne and we're getting out of here as soon as we can.
Monica (*taking his arm*) Perry . . .

There is an ear-splitting scream, off, from Anne. It is followed by another one, then a series of loud bumps and the shattering of china. Then silence. Perry is the first to recover

Perry Anne!

Perry hurries out into the hall

(*Off*) Anne—oh no, *no* . . .!

Dora scuttles to the doorway to peer

(*Off*) *Anne!*
Monica (*unmoving*) What happened, Dora?
Dora (*turning to look at her, horrified*) The Chinese vase. It's *broken.*

With a look of annoyance, Monica moves to the door, edges Dora aside, and exits to the hall

Monica (*as she exits*) Is she dead?
Perry (*off*) I don't know. She's so still.
Monica (*off*) Bring her through here.
Perry (*off*) Is it safe to move her?
Monica (*off*) Well, you can't leave her lying out here. Come on.

After a moment, Dora moves aside to let Perry enter. He carries the still figure of Anne. She is very limp in his arms. Monica enters behind him

Over there.

Perry carries Anne over to the chaise, places her gently on it, then kneels beside her

Perry Oh, Anne. Anne.
Monica (*moving around behind her*) Let me see. (*She lifts up one of Anne's eyelids and peers*) Mhhh. Out cold. (*She releases the lid*)
Perry (*looking up*) How do you exect her to be after falling down those stairs? It's a wonder she wasn't killed.
Monica (*thoughtfully*) Yes. (*She gazes off into the hall*)
Perry (*following her gaze*) What's the matter?
Monica I was just wondering . . . What was it made her scream the *first* time? Before she fell? What had she seen?
Dora (*suddenly*) Oh. (*Her hand goes to her mouth*)
Monica What is it?
Dora (*looking off into the hall*) I've just remembered. That's the exact place Aunt Minerva landed when *she* fell. Broke every bone in her body—and never *touched* that vase. (*She glares at Anne in disapproval*)
Perry (*patting Anne's face with worried vigour*) Anne! Anne! Wake up!
Monica It's no use patting her cheeks like that. The draught'll give her pneumonia. Let's find some smelling-salts.
Dora They didn't help Aunt Minerva. (*She moves to the chaise*)
Monica (*snapping*) Dora!
Dora (*meekly*) I'll go and look for some. (*She steps over Emily and moves to the door*)
Perry Wait.

Dora stops

Don't you think we'd better move Emily before Anne comes round? (*He rises*) It doesn't seem decent to leave her lying there.
Monica (*grudgingly*) All right. We'll shove her next door.
Dora (*surprisedly*) In the dining-room?
Monica I couldn't think of a more fitting place. (*To Perry*) You take her shoulders.

Dora moves back into the room to watch. Perry stoops and takes Emily's shoulders. Monica takes hold of her feet, as Perry heaves, Monica's eyes fix on Anne's legs, and she freezes

Perry (*almost falling over*) Hey?
Monica (*pointing at Anne's leg*) Look.
Perry (*turning to look over his shoulder*) What is it?
Monica (*Leaving Emily, to examine Anne's ankle*) Trip-wire mark. Just starting to come through.
Perry (*releasing Emily's shoulders*) You mean . . .
Monica Somebody intended her to be a Flying Nurse. It must have been stretched across the top of the stairs.
Perry (*examining the mark*) Goes right round the ankle, too. (*He winces*) Nasty.
Monica (*looking again*) Yes. Very nasty. Very nasty indeed.

Anne lets out a low moan

Quick. Let's move this carcass, she's coming round.

Perry and Monica take hold of Emily an stagger out with her

Anne moans again. Dora looks off then sidles over to Anne's side

Anne (*weakly*) Perry.
Dora (*looking off again*) It's all right, dear. *I*'ll look after you.
Anne (*beginning to come round*) Perry.
Dora Want to see your Mister Potter, do you, dear? Want to have a *talk* to him, perhaps?
Anne (*her head rolling*) Perry.
Dora (*smiling*) Well, we don't want that, do we? Not while you're delirious. There's no knowing *what* you might say, is there? (*She glances over at the door again*) Perhaps I'd better make you a little more comfortable? (*She picks up a cushion*) Now just lie still . . .

Dora begins to approach Anne's head, gently lowering the cushion. Anne's eyes suddenly open and see her

Anne (*drowsy*) What . . .? (*She realizes*) No. (*She screams*) Perry! (*With a desperate, one-armed push, she sends Dora reeling back and struggles to sit up*)
Dora (*panic-stricken*) Shhhh! Shhhh!
Anne (*shouting*) Perry!

Perry and Monica come hurrying in

Perry Anne. (*He hurries to her*)
Anne (*sobbing*) She was trying to kill me. She was going to smother me with the cushion. (*She buries her head into Perry's shoulder*) Oh, Perry.
Dora (*holding out the cushion*) I was putting it under her head to make her more comfortable.
Monica (*drily*) Well, at least we've added another bit of useful knowledge to our memory cells. A cushion makes a good substitute for smelling salts. (*She takes the cushion from Dora and tosses it down*) Are you all right?
Anne (*fighting back the tears*) I think so. I'm hurting all over. My leg . . .

Perry Let me see. (*He touches her leg below the knee*)

Anne gives a sharp gasp of pain and bites her lip

Oh! I—I think it's broken.
Monica Broken?
Anne (*weakly*) Let me . . .

Perry helps her to sit up again. She gingerly probes her leg, then cries out

Ohhh! (*She slumps*) Oh, yes. Yes. (*She gasps*) Oh, Perry . . .
Perry Don't worry. We'll get you to a doctor. The fog's starting to clear.
Anne (*clutching him*) You're not going to leave me here? Alone?
Monica Don't worry. You're quite safe now. We know exactly who's behind all this, and from now on we're going to be working together.
Anne (*looking from one to the other*) You—know?
Monica Of course. It's our supposedly late unlamented Papa. He's the only one it can be.
Dora (*bridling*) I don't know how you can say that, Monica. I refuse to listen.
Anne (*shaking her head*) You're wrong, Monica. It's not your father.
Dora I should think not indeed.
Monica It must be. That trip-wire wasn't across the stairs when you went up them, or you'd have noticed it. Therefore it must have been put there *after* you'd passed. Now none of *us* left this room, and the rest of them are dead. *Ergo*—our mysterious murderer *must* be Papa.
Perry (*wide-eyed*) Of course. You're absolutely right.
Anne (*still shaking her head*) She isn't. He's lying upstairs on my bedroom floor. He fell out of the wardrobe when I opened it to get my coat. (*She shudders*) That's why I screamed. It was so unexpected.

There is a stunned silence

Monica (*slowly*) So that means I'm wrong again. There's somebody else in the house.
Anne (*almost in a whisper*) What are we going to do?
Perry (*holding her tightly*) It's all right, Anne. It's all right. (*To Monica*) Well, that looks like that. We can't risk going for a doctor now.
Monica We'll have to stay here until help comes to *us*.
Anne (*horrified*) But that could take *months*.
Monica Even years. Nobody comes here these days unless it's by accident. The local tradesmen dump everything at the gates and she—(*indicating Anne*)—goes into the village once a month to settle up with them. None of the family have left here for years.
Dora Except Marcus, of course. But he didn't know any better, did he? And they always brought him back.
Perry Who did?
Monica Penworthy and her. (*She indicates Anne again*)
Dora He was very fond of Mr Penworthy. He sounded so like Father, you see, and poor Marcus was very short-sighted. I often wondered why he

didn't wear spectacles, but I suppose they didn't have them in Roman times, so of course he wouldn't, would he?

Perry (*sighing*) Well. This is just marvellous, isn't it? Here we are, stuck in this crazy old building with one of us injured, six dead bodies, and an unknown maniac stalking the rest of us, having a cosy little chat about short-sighted Romans. The only thing we're short of now is an old-fashioned thunderstorm and a blasted power failure.

There is a flicker and the Lights go out

Me and my big mouth.

Anne (*afraid*) Perry . . .!

The Lights fade in again

Dora (*wide-eyed*) It's the generator. Somebody's tampering with it.

The Lights fade out again

Monica (*sharply*) Nobody move. Stay right where you are.

Perry But there's somebody out there.

Monica It's probably just run out of fuel. There's nothing to worry about. We've got a spare one on standby. I'll fix it.

Anne No. We can build up the fire. It may be a trap.

Monica I can take care of myself.

Monica exits to the hall

Dora Monica. Don't! I'm frightened.

Anne Perry. Stop her.

Perry I can't see a thing.

There is a bump and a thud as something is knocked over

Ouch. Monica?

There is another bump

Oooh. (*He sucks in a breath*)

Anne Are you all right?

Perry (*tightly*) Yes.

Anne (*suddenly*) Perry—where are you?

Perry Over here.

Anne (*strained*) Don't move. Stand still.

Perry What is it?

Anne I can feel a draught on the back of my neck. I think the panel's opened. (*Pause*) There's somebody in the room with us.

Perry What?

Anne They're right behind me. (*Getting hysterical*) Perry! Light a match. Light a match, quickly!

Perry (*panic-stricken*) I don't smoke. I haven't got one!

Anne (*her voice rising*) The fire! Poke the fire! (*She screams*) No! No! Perry! Help me! (*She screams again*)

Perry (*calling*) I can't find you!

There is a confused jumble of bumps and thumps, as Perry blunders around. Anne's screams are cut off abruptly

(*Relieved*) Anne. It's all right. I've got you. I'm right here. I'm right beside you.

The Lights suddenly flash on again. Anne is lying prostrate on the chaise. Perry is on his knees in front of Dora, who is sitting in the wing-chair, his arms wrapped tightly about her legs. The secret panel is wide open. As Perry realizes who he is holding, he quickly releases her and scrambles to his feet. The movement causes Dora to topple forward. She has been strangled with her own scarf

(*Recoiling*) Aaaaah! (*He pushes Dora back into the chair and looks round for Anne*) Anne? (*He sees her and rushes to her side*) Anne . . .

As he stoops over her, Anne springs into life, clutching hold of him and screaming loudly

Anne. No. No it's me. Shhhh! Shhhhh!

Anne (*realizing*) Oh. Oh, Perry. Perry. (*She breaks into sobs*)

Suddenly Anne spots Dora and stiffens. Perry quickly moves his body to obstruct her gaze

Perry Don't look.

Anne (*stunned*) And I thought it was *her*. (*She clings to him*) Ohhhhh!

Perry It's all right.

Anne (*pulling herself together*) Then it was Monica. It was Monica all the time. I felt her brushing past me. I *tried* to hold on to her, but she was too strong.

There is the sound of mocking laughter from Monica inside the secret passage. They both turn in shock

She's mad. Stark staring mad.

The laughter rings out again, then the panel silently closes, cutting off the sound

Perry (*after a short silence*) What are we going to do now?

Anne (*defeated*) What *can* we do? We haven't a chance without that gun. She must have taken it while we were moving Agatha. We're done for.

Perry (*determinedly*) Not yet, we aren't. I can carry you down to the village.

Anne (*shaking her head*) You'd never manage it. Not that distance. And I couldn't stand the pain. I'm sorry.

Perry There must be *something*. Let me think. (*He catches sight of Dora again, winces, then moves over to her and turns the chair upstage to face the window*) Sorry about that, but she was making me nervous. Now where was I? (*He remembers*) Oh, yes. Got it. The *entrances*. Seal all the entrances. That'll stop her. (*He gets hold of the table*)

Anne Perry.

He ignores her but tugs heartily

Perry. What's the use? We're not going to get out of here alive, and you know it. She's got us trapped.
Perry Not if I've got anything to do with it.
Anne Our only chance is to get her before she can get us.
Perry (*nodding*) Right. (*He spots the family Bible*) Ah, the very thing. That should give her a nasty headache.
Anne (*puzzled*) What are you going to do?
Perry (*moving to the Bible table*) Balance this over the door. Then when she tries to come in—boof. (*He picks up the Bible, moves towards the door, then trips and falls down*) Oooof! (*The book thuds to the floor and opens*) Hey . . . (*He scrabbles at it*)
Anne What is it?

Perry holds up the gun

Perry It was hidden inside this book. Somebody's cut a space out.
Anne (*excitedly*) Is it loaded?
Perry (*looking*) Just the one bullet left.
Anne (*laughing with relief*) Then we've got her. We're saved. Oh, Perry. We're safe.

Monica's laugh floats in from the hall

Monica (*off, singing*)
Three green bottles, hanging on the wall.
Three green bottles, hanging on the wall.
And if one green bottle, should accidently fall,
There'll be two green bottles, hanging on the wall.
(*Spoken*) Did you hear that, Perry, baby. *Two* green bottles. With lots and lots of lovely money to split between them. How's about it, Perry? Do you want to make a deal?
Anne (*hissing*) Don't listen to her.
Monica (*off, singing*) Two green bottles, hanging on the wall . . .
Anne Perry . . .!
Monica (*off*) Two green bottles, hanging on the wall . . .
Anne (*covering her ears*) Stop her! Stop her!
Monica (*off, singing*)
And if one green bottle should accidently fall,
There'll be——
(*Startled*) Ooh! *You!* But it can't be. You're dead. (*Her voice rises*) No! Keep away from me! Perry—help me! Help me! (*She screams in terror*)

Anne lowers her hands, startled. Perry stands dumbstruck. There is a moment of complete silence

Perry (*cautiously*) Monica? (*Silence*) Monica??

The house is silent. Perry looks at Anne

Anne (*almost in a whisper*) It's a trick. It *has* to be.
Perry Do—do you think I should—take a look?
Anne No. It's a trap. She's trying to separate us. I *know* she is.

Perry (*uncertainly*) But she said there was someone out there. Someone who's supposed to be dead.
Anne There *couldn't* be. We've seen all the bodies.

Perry moves to the door

Perry. Come back! Don't leave me! (*She tries to sit up*)
Perry (*looking back at her*) I've got to be sure.

Perry exits

Anne looks after him in frustration

(*Off*) Monica? Are you there?

As Anne looks off, the panel behind her opens and Monica appears holding a long knife. She moves down behind Anne and raises the knife to stab. With a swift movement, her arm encircles Anne's neck, pulling back her head and the knife flashes down

Anne (*screaming*) No . . .!

Anne's hand flies up and grabs Monica's wrist. Laughing madly, Monica wrestles with her, Anne still shouts for help

Perry! Perry!

Perry dashes into the room and sees them. Quickly he raises the gun and points it at Monica

Perry Monica! (*He threatens her*)

Monica looks up and laughs, then continues the struggle. Perry closes his eyes, holds out the gun and fires. Monica jolts upright, half turns with a look of surprise on her face, then crumples in a heap. Anne collapses sobbing. Perry drops the gun and hurries to her

Anne!
Anne (*sobbing*) I told you she was faking. I *told* you.
Perry (*holding her and looking at Monica*) Poor Monica. She must have wanted that money pretty badly.
Anne (*clinging to him*) But to commit *murder* . . . (*She sobs*)
Perry (*sadly*) And all for nothing, too.
Anne (*wiping away her tears*) Nothing? There were four million pounds at stake.
Perry (*gently*) Anne. There's something I've got to tell you—and I don't know quite how to do it. You see—the truth of the matter is—well—it's all been a ghastly mistake. All these murders. They needn't have happened at all.
Anne (*baffled*) I don't understand.
Perry (*getting more embarrassed*) What I'm trying to say is—it's all my fault. You see—I'm the one who's been responsible for killing everybody.
Anne (*stunned*) *You?* (*Her hand goes to her mouth*)

Perry (*quickly*) Oh, I don't mean *personally*. But it's all my fault they got murdered. It's because I'm so painfully *shy*. Always have been, in fact. And when you said that Freda had been murdered because that was the only way the Tomb family could get hold of the money—it made me feel terrible. Because if I hadn't been too embarrassed to tell the truth about myself, she needn't have died at all.

Anne Truth?

Perry Ermyntrude Ash wasn't Freda at all. She's me.

Anne (*surprised*) *You?*

Perry (*nodding*) I'd always wanted to be a writer, you see, but the only things I could write well were romantic novels for women. And I couldn't write that sort of thing under my own name, or I'd have been laughed out of my job. (*Looking down*) I'm an undertaker's assistant to Grimly and Welldug's. (*He looks up again*) We thought it best for me to stay on there so nobody would get suspicious. Freda was my agent. The only other person who knew my secret. So when I was supposed to give interviews, and do fêtes and things—she came along too and pretended to be me.

Anne I see.

Perry (*earnestly*) I know I should have said something before, but I wasn't too sure what was happening—and with Freda dying like that, well . . . (*Hesitantly*) You don't mind do you? Honestly?

Anne Mind? Oh, Perry, I'm *delighted* for you. That means the money's really yours. Four million pounds. Oh . . . (*She hugs him*)

Perry But I'm not going to *keep* it. Not after what's happened. I'll give it all to charity, if we ever find it. I couldn't *bear* to touch it.

Anne (*amused*) Then I think *I*'d better handle it. After all—charity begins at home.

Perry (*stubbornly*) I'm not interested. (*He moves away*) It's caused the deaths of too many people. Let it do some good for a change.

Anne It can do *us* good, Perry.

Perry I don't want it.

Anne (*incredulously*) And do you think I'm going to stand by and watch you throw a fortune away as if it were nothing?

Perry It is nothing—to me. (*He turns to face her*) And besides—you're not going to be doing any standing for some time. Not with that broken leg of yours.

Anne looks at him silently for a moment, then with a deliberate movement, swings her legs to the floor and stands

Anne (*coldly*) You were saying?

Perry gapes at her

That's the worst of some people. They'll believe anything you want them to if you make it sound convincing. (*She moves towards him*)

Perry (*backing away slightly*) You—you're walking.

Anne (*stopping and smiling at him*) How very observant of you, darling. What a pity your brain isn't as sharp as your eyes. (*With great venom*)

You poor fool. I didn't plan all this just to see that cash slip through my fingers because of *your* high moral standards. That money is *mine* and I'm going to have it. Understand, darling?

Perry (*flat against the wall*) It was *you*! It was you all along.

Anne (*easily*) With a little help from the late Mr Penworthy. Oh, yes. He was in on it too. (*Waving a hand*) Do stop clutching that wall like a sprig of ivy. I'm not going to harm *you*. Sit down and relax while I tell you the rest of the story, I'm sure you'll find it fascinating. (*She moves to the drinks table and pours herself a drink*) Cheers. (*She lifts the glass to him and sips*) Now where was I? (*She frowns*) Do sit *down*, Perry. You're making me feel nervous.

Perry remains glued to the wall

SIT!

Perry hurriedly moves to the desk chair and sits

That's better. (*She takes another sip*) Well, the first thing we had to do was to get me into the family without raising anyone's suspicions. They had very nasty minds, the Tombs. (*She smiles*) Poor Marcus. We'd only to convince him that Caesar should have a wife, and the rest was easy.

Perry (*suddenly*) Calphurnia.

Anne Pardon?

Perry Caesar's wife. That's what he called you. Calphurnia.

Anne Oh—yes. He nearly gave the game away there, didn't he? We never expected anyone in *this* house to see the connection. (*She laughs*) The poor fool. He didn't need much persuading to slip away in secret and meet us at the registry office in Town. Penworthy acted as a witness for us. We had the certificate tucked away in a safe place just waiting to be produced on cue. (*She smiles*) As sole surviving member of the Tomb family, I'd inherit the whole fortune. Pretty neat, eh?

Perry Except for one thing.

Anne Yes. We never expected you to turn up incognito. It was very naughty of you, Peregrine. You caused us to get rid of the wrong Miss Ash. Still . . . (*With a light laugh*) If we'd known about your little secret a bit sooner, we might have poisoned *you* instead. I can't tell you what a shock you gave us when you suddenly came back. Penworthy wanted to call the whole thing off—but I forced him to go on. Oliver was easy. Well, fairly so. He would keep trying to avoid being hit. That's why Penworthy had to use so many bullets. In the meantime, I exercised my talents by cutting the telephone wires. (*She sips her drink*)

Perry I don't want to hear any more.

Anne (*ignoring him*) Of course, it gave *me* something to think about when Penworthy got knifed. Monica was right. He'd not gone down to the village at all. He'd gone out there to finish you off. Not for any particular reason, you understand, but you were a loose end that needed tidying. You do see that, don't you?

Perry I suppose so.

Anne And if that sex-mad cow—(*indicating Monica*)—hadn't poked her nose in, he'd have done it, too. Still—it was all for the best. I'd have had to dispose of him myself later on. I didn't intend sharing my life and fortune with Mr Hamilton Penworthy, thank you very much. But I was badly worried at the time. There was someone else in on the act, and I'd no idea who it was.

Perry My heart bleeds for you.

Anne (*smiling*) I'm sure it's going to. (*Briskly*) I had to work fast. I remembered that Penworthy had the marriage certificate down here, and sent Marcus to look for it. Of course, I followed him by way of the passageways. (*She muses*) I suppose I *should* have used a knife on him, but the gun made a louder noise. (*Brightly*) I wanted someone in here to help prove my innocence when the body was found. Clever, eh?

Perry Diabolical.

Anne (*nodding*) It was all worked out to the last detail. Even to the charade of trying to save his life when I knew he was as dead as a dodo. No-one argues with a nurse over a dying patient, do they? Lucien was easy. I'd already lured him away from here by telling him that somebody had wrecked his precious laboratory. I got him less than a minute after shooting Marcus. He never even knew what hit him. And then came Agatha. The good and faithful servant. *Too* faithful for my liking. I hadn't realized she'd overheard Penworthy and myself plotting until she mentioned that she'd heard old man Tomb's voice in here. Dora was right. He sounded just like Old Septimus at times. Of course, I had to get rid of her, too. Not only because she might have recognized *my* voice, and put the knife into Penworthy, but because *you* told me she'd got hold of that marriage certificate, and I knew it wouldn't take her long to start putting two and two together. (*She sips*) She should never have hung that meat-axe by the kitchen door. It was a like a gift from the gods.

Perry (*stunned*) I can't believe it. How can you be so cold blooded?

Anne Practice makes perfect. (*She moves to the drinks table to pour another drink*) Besides—when one has assisted at as many operations as I have, a little blood and bone doesn't worry you overmuch. Of course, when Monica admitted it was *she* who'd done for Penworthy, I almost gave the game away with relief. But I knew now what had happened, I knew it would all be plain sailing. I threw my big scene and cleared off to collect Lucien's head, then waited in the passage for the room to clear.

Perry But you couldn't have done. I was outside your door.

Anne (*patiently*) One can also *exit* by a secret passageway, my pet. Why do you think I locked the door in your face? I couldn't risk you coming in and finding the room empty, could I? (*She moves to the fireplace*) It didn't take much ingenuity to lure Dora into the passageway, and it only took me a minute to slip back and help you look for her. (*She sips*) Emily was the easiest. I'd injected that apple with cyanide the previous evening. I knew it would only be a matter of time before she sank her little white fangs into it, and the beauty of it was, I didn't have to be anywhere near her at the time.

Perry But you tried to save her.

Anne (*laughing*) There's no cure for cyanide, darling. Of course I tried to save her. I had to make it look good. (*She muses*) You know—I've often thought I should have been an actress. Can you see me as another Sarah Bernhardt?

Perry You're more like Lady Macbeth.

Anne (*chuckling*) Naughty. (*She sips*) Then at that point I made a mistake. Oh, yes. I admit it. I'd removed the only reason to keep me here. Marcus *was* dead, and the fog was beginning to lift. I noticed it before I ran out of here. Hence the fall downstairs. Naturally, I didn't *actually* fall. I just fixed up the trip-wire I'd prepared for Dora, pulled it tightly around my ankle to make a mark, arranged the old man's body on my bedroom floor—oh yes, we'd moved him a few days ago—then knocked over the vase and arranged myself amidst the fragments. All very artistic and convincing. With a broken leg—diagnosed by myself—we had no choice but to stay on.

Perry But you were unconscious. Monica examined you.

Anne Did you think I wouldn't have expected that? I didn't underestimate the way her mind worked. I gave myself a small jab with the needle. Just enough to knock me out for a few minutes. It was simple. As simple as opening the tap on the generator's fuel tank to make the lights fail while you were all in here earlier. (*She looks over at Dora*) Poor Dora. Such a scraggy neck. So fragile. By the time it got down to you or Monica—in your own minds that is—she had to turn killer again to save her own skin. What a good job it was that you discovered where she'd hidden the gun. She almost outsmarted me there. But you got her didn't you, Perry. *You* got her.

Perry Eh? (*He looks puzzled*)

Anne Your fingerprints are on the gun, darling. Just waiting for some eager little policeman with big feet to notice them.

Perry suddenly realizes and makes a move for it

Naughty, naughty. (*She picks up the poker*) Mustn't destroy the evidence must we?

Perry Evidence?

Anne That you did the murders. (*She shrugs regretfully*) We have to blame *somebody*.

Perry They'll never believe it.

Anne Oh, I assure you they will. Three bodies with bullets in them and your fingerprints all over the gun. They'll be only too willing to believe. I wouldn't be surprised if they don't think you killed all the others too. Especially when I've finished telling my story.

Perry And what's that?

Anne That you came here at the invitation of Monica—under an assumed name—and managed to kill off almost everybody in the household before you fell out with her. You beat her to the draw, but fortunately poor little me managed to escape and knock you out with this before calling for the police. (*She smiles*) I'll work out all the details on the way into the village.

Perry And do you honestly think you're going to get away with it?

Anne I don't see why not, darling. I can be very convincing.

Perry Then I'll tell you. (*More firmly*) You made *another* mistake Anne. A very big one.

Anne (*in mock surprise*) I did? You must tell me.

Perry (*pointing*) I will. The mark around your ankle.

Anne (*frowning slightly*) What about it?

Perry If somebody falls over a trip-wire like you're supposed to have done—then they only get a mark where *the wire actually touches*. It doesn't go all the way round the ankle. Monica spotted it at once. She pointed it out to me when we took Emily's body next door.

Anne (*her eyes smouldering*) How very *astute* of her.

Perry Wasn't it? And not very clever of you. As soon as the police see that mark, you'll be done for. They'll know you're lying.

Anne Well, well, well. What a nasty conniving person you really are, Mr Potter. So you knew all along?

Perry I wasn't convinced. I just couldn't understand how you'd managed it. I had to hear it for myself. I'm just sorry it wasn't in time to save poor Dora.

Anne Not forgetting the clever Miss Monica, who so kindly supplied us with her own murder weapon. (*She laughs*) I bet that gave her a shock.

Perry But nothing to the shock *you're* going to get. Monica isn't dead. I missed her by a mile. She's heard everything we've said, and between us we've got you cornered. (*He calls*) You can get up now.

With a snarl of rage, Anne turns to look at Monica—who remains motionless on the floor

Monica? (*He gulps*) Monica! Get up. We've got her. *Monica??*

Anne gives a harsh laugh and turns to look at Perry

Anne Something seems to have gone wrong, doesn't it, *darling*? You really have killed her. (*She laughs again*)

Perry (*scuttling to Monica's side*) Monica. (*He shakes her*) Monica!

Anne (*sweetly*) I can see I'll have to change my plans a little. I can't have you pointing out my ankle to those nasty old detectives, can I? (*She moves towards him*) They might be inclined to listen to you. (*She raises the poker*)

Perry backs away from her

It's no use backing away from me, darling. This is going to hurt you far more than it will me. I'll just have to finish you off as well. Fighting for my life against a vicious killer. I'm sure no-one will find it in their hearts to blame me. (*She lashes out*)

Perry (*dodging*) Help! (*He dashes away*) Help!

Anne (*cutting him off*) There's no-one going to hear you, darling. No-one at all. (*She lashes out madly again*)

Perry dodges again and grabs her arm. Anne snarls with rage and they wrestle for the poker. Monica suddenly rolls over and springs to her feet at the sight of them. With a swift movement she rams her knife into Anne's back

Monica *Et tu, Brute.*

All three are frozen into immobility. Anne half turns, then crumples to the floor, dead

Perry (*gasping*) Ohhhhh! Ohhhhh!
Monica (*brushing her forehead*) Sorry about that. But you almost gave me a new parting with that bullet. I nearly didn't make it.
Perry (*panting*) Neither did I.
Monica (*sympathetically*) Poor Perry. But you played that last scene like Laurence Olivier. I could never have managed it without you. If she hadn't tried to be so clever with that trip-wire, she could have finished us all off. Thank goodness you caught on so fast when I pointed it out. She walked straight into our trap.
Perry But not soon enough to save poor Dora.
Monica No. But soon enough to save us—and the missing millions.
Perry Please. I never want to hear about that awful money again. Let it stay hidden forever.
Monica But I know where it is.
Perry (*startled*) You do?
Monica (*producing a slip of paper*) I found this inside the passageways a few minutes ago. We must have been walking over it for weeks.
Perry What is it?
Monica A confirmation note from your publishers, acknowledging order and payment in advance for two million copies of your latest book *Passion in Cheltenham* at two pounds per copy. To be delivered on request.
Perry (*dazed*) Two million copies? At two pounds each? Four million pounds (*He sits at the desk*) That explains why these bookshelves are empty. He was waiting for *my* books.
Monica (*moving in to him*) So that's that. You'll get part of your fortune after all—if only in royalties.
Perry (*tiredly*) I suppose we'd better get the police.
Monica (*getting even closer*) Let them wait. A few hours more won't make much difference. (*She presses close to him*)
Perry (*leaning back*) Few hours?
Monica (*toying with him*) Well—we're all alone now. There's no-one to disturb us. (*She begins to play with his shirt buttons*)
Perry (*rising awkwardly*) Now wait a minute, Monica . . .
Monica (*pulling off his tie*) We've got plenty of time to get a little more—friendly towards each other.
Perry No. Wait. (*He backs away*) Monica. Listen.
Monica (*trying to slide his shirt off*) Peregrine.
Perry (*struggling free*) Monica. No! Help! (*He dashes away*) Help!
Monica (*chasing him*) Perry baby. Perreeeeeeee . . .

Perry races round the room frantically with Monica in pursuit, as—

the CURTAIN *falls*

FURNITURE AND PROPERTY LIST

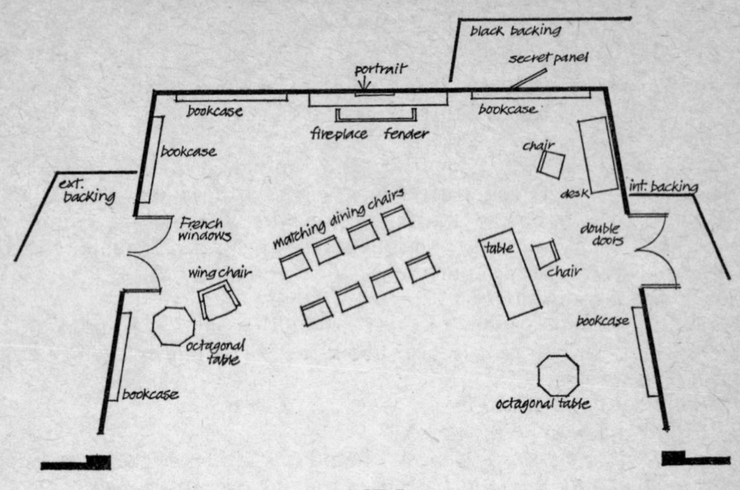

ACT I

On stage: Wing-chair
Desk chair

Library chair
8 matched dining-chairs
Library table. *On it:* cigarette-box
Octagonal drinks table. *On it:* several cut-glass decanters with various brightly coloured liquids, various glasses and goblets
Octagonal matching table. *On it:* family Bible with pages cut to secrete gun
Roll-top desk. *In it:* blotter, quill pens, papers, inks. *In pigeon-holes:* papers. *On floor:* loose envelopes. *Below it:* wastepaper-basket
All round walls: empty, mesh-covered bookshelves: one concealing secret panel
Carved wood fender
Fire-dogs, poker, tongs, logs
On mantelpiece: 2 large vases, ornate clock
Over mantel: portrait of Septimus Tomb
Thick carpet
Velvet drapes and coffee-coloured net curtains
Hearthrug

Off stage: Battered deeds box containing Will and papers (**Penworthy**)
Letter (**Penworthy**)
Steel dish with syringe and swabs (**Anne**)
Spare syringe and swabs (**Anne**)

Personal: **Penworthy:** gold turnip-watch, fob, chain
Emily: apple

ACT II

Scene 1

Off stage:	Blanket, bath towel **(Agatha)** Suit shirt, underclothing **(Monica)** Gun on pencil **(Penworthy)** **Penworthy**'s coat and scarf **(Agatha)** Trick kitchen knife **(Penworthy)**
Personal:	**Emily:** apple

Scene 2

Strike:	Dirty glasses and glass from floor Dining-chairs
Set:	Window curtains open Chaise-longue in place of dining-chairs. *On it:* cushion
Off stage:	Blood-stained meat-axe **(Agatha)** Dressing **(Perry)** Towels, blanket, bowl of water, first-aid box **(Agatha)** "Blood" bowl and sponge **(Anne)** Large cardboard box with masses of tissue paper **(Dora)**
Personal:	**Emily:** sandwich

ACT III

Strike:	"Head" box and tissue paper Blanket, towels, bowl of water
Set:	Gun in Bible Papers back in deeds box Dish of apples on library table
Off stage:	Plateful of thick sandwiches **(Perry)** Knife **(Monica)** Slip of paper **(Monica)**

LIGHTING PLOT

Property fittings required: chandelier, wall brackets, log fire effect
Interior: A library. The same scene throughout

ACT I. Evening
To open: Practicals and log fire on
No cues

ACT II, SCENE 1. Evening
To open: As Scene 1
No cues

ACT II, SCENE 2. Morning
To open: General effect of weak, foggy daylight. Fire on
No cues

ACT III. Evening
To open: As Act I, SCENE 1 Fire lit, but low

Cue 1 **Perry**: "... and a blasted power failure." (Page 62)
Lights flicker and go out

Cue 2 **Anne**: "Perry ...!" (Page 62)
Lights come up again

Cue 3 **Dora**: "... tampering with it." (Page 62)
Lights fade to Black-out

Cue 4 **Perry**: "I'm right beside you." (Page 63)
Lights flash back on

EFFECTS PLOT

ACT I

Cue 1	As CURTAIN rises *Internal telephone rings, then stops. Wolf howls*	(Page 1)
Cue 2	**Penworthy** warms hands *Wolf howls*	(Page 2)
Cue 3	**Penworthy.** ". . . wherever you may be." *Wolf howls*	(Page 2)
Cue 4	**Penworthy:** ". . . to full moon." *Wolf howls*	(Page 2)
Cue 5	**Emily:** ". . . thinking he's a werewolf . . ." *Wolf howls*	(Page 7)
Cue 6	**Emily:** "I'll tell you . . ." *Loud knock on outer door*	(Page 12)
Cue 7	**Emily:** ". . . paid for, isn't it?" *Sound of rusty bolts and hinges*	(Page 12)
Cue 8	**Perry:** "Thank you." *Sound of door closing*	(Page 12)
Cue 9	**Freda:** "Very carefully indeed." *Wolf howls*	(Page 16)

ACT II

SCENE 1

Cue 10	**Emily:** "Fetch her." *Hammering on outer door*	(Page 26)
Cue 11	**Penworthy:** "Agatha." *Sound of rusty bolts and hinges*	(Page 26)
Cue 12	**Perry:** "Get off. Let go!" *Three revolver shots*	(Page 30)
Cue 13	**Perry:** "I'll come with you." *Revolver shot*	(Page 38)

SCENE 2

Cue 14	**Lucien:** ". . . absolute fortunes—disgraceful." *Internal telephone rings*	(Page 43)

ACT III

Cue 15	**Monica:** "Perry." **Anne** screams *Loud bumps and china crash*	(Page 58)

MADE AND PRINTED IN GREAT BRITAIN BY
LATIMER TREND & COMPANY LTD PLYMOUTH
MADE IN ENGLAND